Electronic collection development
A practical guide

By the same author

Digital imaging: a practical handbook

Electronic collection development
A practical guide

Stuart D. Lee

NEAL-SCHUMAN PUBLISHERS INC.
NEW YORK
IN ASSOCIATION WITH
LIBRARY ASSOCIATION PUBLISHING, LONDON

Published by
Neal-Schuman Publishers, Inc.
100 Varick Street
New York, NY 10013

ISBN 1-55570-440-9

Published simultaneously with Library Association Publishing, London.
Printed and made in Great Britain.

Contents

Acknowledgements

This book would not have been possible without all the support and help I have received over the years from the various members of Oxford University's Datasets Committee. Although they are too numerous to mention I owe them all a big debt of gratitude. As always I am indebted to my colleagues at the Humanities Computing Unit at Oxford, for their seemingly infinite wisdom. I would also like to acknowledge all the help and support I have received from colleagues on the JIBS User Group (**http://hosted.ukoln.ac.uk/jibs/**). In addition I would like to personally thank Adrian Hale and Alun Edwards (Oxford University) for their help and guidance with reference to cataloguing issues, and also all of the following who helped out with individual requests throughout the writing of this book: Liz Chapman, Oxford University; Grazyna Cooper, Oxford University; Bridget Lewis, Oxford University; Cliff McKnight, Loughborough University; Ann Okerson, Yale University; Sarah Porter, JISC; Margaret Robb, Oxford University; John Smith, University of Kent; Barbara Tearle, University of Oxford; Greg Walker, Oxford University; Alicia Wise, JISC.

1 Preliminary issues

The development of new carriers for the storage of information, traditionally produced on paper, has brought about a fundamental change in thinking within national libraries about future collection policies and storage requirements and an awareness that in order to maintain comprehensive collections of national publications for present and future generations of users, it will be necessary to obtain an increasing amount of non-print material.

(*The legal deposit of electronic publications*, Working Group of the Conference of Directors of National Libraries (UNESCO, 1996, **www.unesco.org/webworld/memory/legaldep.htm**)

Background

The history of the 'dataset' (the term is explained in the next section) is, in a sense, as old as the earliest library or mankind's first attempt to store and order data. Up until World War 2 the goal had been to make the best and most profitable use of one medium – the codex. Efforts were centred on the compilation, distribution, and referencing of the printed or handwritten work. For authors and readers alike, the internal structure of the book had been the subject of continued development, and readers witnessed the appearance of numerous navigational aids (for example, indexes, tables of contents, footnotes, annotated editions, and cross-referencing). Publishers too had been focusing entirely on this one area – the printing, marketing, and selling of the paper-based medium.

Yet in the space of 50 years this has all changed. Prior to the 1940s there had been primitive dabblings with the storage, manipulation, and searching of material held in electronic form (in truth relying more on mechanical systems than anything truly 'digital'), but the years from 1939 to 1945 saw landmark projects, such as those at Britain's Bletchley Park, which demonstrated the power of the computer to handle and process vast amounts of material with speed. It is interesting to note that one of the first non-military applications of this technology began to take place only shortly after the end of the war, with Father Roberto Busa's project on the works of St Thomas Aquinas (the *Index Thomisticus* initiated in 1946).

The American Chemical Society began alerting scholars to new developments through electronic means as far back as 1962. Batch offline files began appearing a few years later, and *Chemical Biological Activities* appeared in 1965 both in print and on tape. In 1971 MEDLINE (Medical Literature Online) was launched and Project Gutenberg (**www.promo. net/pg/**) issued its first electronic text (*The Declaration of Independence*). Outside of the hard sciences, to anyone charged with collection development (be they publisher or librarian), and to the end-users or readers themselves, most of the activities up to the mid-1980s seemed interesting but in the main irrelevant to their everyday work. However, the signs were there that this would all change. As far back as 1972 the large commercial organizations which focused on electronic publications (e.g. Dialog and ORBIT) came into view, and LEXIS appeared in 1973. The writing was on the wall, so to speak, that this was to be an emerging technology that would be applicable to all subjects in all sectors.

Since then the world seems to have exploded in a shower of digital products and technological advances. In the early 1990s it became for the first time cheaper to publish a reference work on CD-ROM than it did in print format. Undoubtedly all of this has had important implications for the way businesses, academics, publishers, and readers get access to information essential for their work. Most importantly for librarians, or collection development officers, entirely new markets have rapidly evolved. To put it in perspective, in the space of a few years we have collectively witnessed in electronic format the appearance of all the major reference titles for most subject areas, a process that originally took several hundred years to complete in the print world.

F. W. Lancaster (1995) outlined a brief history of electronic publishing in which he saw:

1. Use of computers to generate conventional print-on-paper publications . . .
2. The distribution of text in electronic form, where the electronic version is the exact equivalent of a paper version and may have been used to generate the paper version . . .
3. Distribution in electronic form only but with the publication being little more than print on paper displayed electronically. Nevertheless, it may have various 'value added' features, including search, data manipulation and alerting (through profile matching) capabilities.
4. The generation of completely new publications that exploit the true capabilities of electronics (e.g. hypertext and hypermedia, electronic analog models, motion, sound).

At present it is safe to say that all four modes of operation are being employed. However, to collection developers attempting to build up a selection of electronic resources, the material generated by 2, 3, and 4 are of the most importance. They must not only consider the range of titles produced by commercial publishers, but also develop strategies which allow them to cope with all these products. To exacerbate the problem in most institutions the purchasing of electronic resources cannot be viewed in isolation from traditional collection development strategies (indeed, as we will see, publishers still talk about the duality of print and electronic material). Many of the lessons learnt over the years by librarians involved in purchasing printed material should not be forgotten as soon as we move to the digital arena. More importantly, with many of the deals on offer (notable in the area of electronic journals and electronic books, discussed in Chapter 3) there is an explicit link between print and electronic subscriptions.

This book is aimed at the librarian, collection developer, or student who is interested in looking at the range of electronic resources available, how they might be evaluated, and the whole process of purchasing such titles. In addition this book will be of interest to publishers who are beginning to explore this supposedly lucrative area.

What is a dataset?

The term 'dataset' is used throughout this book as a general nomenclature for any electronic resource that has been published with an aim to being marketed. Although there are many vexing questions about the wealth of material that is freely available on the web (in terms of its validity and usability), the main focus of this book is the product that is presented to the collection developer for sale or subscription. By this definition, therefore, the term does not cover the purchasing of applications or software via a site licence but rather something that contains preordained content. However, that said, some of the issues surrounding the evaluation of 'paid for' products overlap considerably with the criteria one would use to assess a free product containing content (i.e. a freely accessible website), and therefore the issues outlined in Chapter 4 are of generic use.

It has to be recognized that elsewhere the term 'dataset' has connotations of numerical data in some discussions, but here when discussing datasets we are referring to full textbases, electronic journals, image collections, other multimedia products, and of course collections of numerical data. These may be delivered on CD-ROM, on tape, via the internet, and so on. In this context then the term means:

> Any electronic product that delivers a collection of data, be it text, numerical, graphical, or time based, as a commercially available title.

The latter comment is in many ways the more interesting. Because it has the potential to be marketed, one can surmise that there must be at the one end a supplier and at the other a potential pool of consumers. For the most part the large electronic publications that have appeared are aimed at research and teaching institutions, and therefore the librarian, or the person charged with developing collections, is the 'consumer'. Yet this is not always the case. One of the quickest growing areas in the datasets world is that of business and economic information, where the market consists mainly of commercial firms rather than academic institutions.

Overall then, the term dataset as used in this book is similar to the International Coalition of Library Consortia's definition of 'e-information':

A broad term that encompasses abstracting and indexing services, electronic journals and other full text materials, the offerings of information aggregators, article delivery services, etc. E-information can be accessed via remote networks from information providers, or locally mounted by a consortium or one of its member libraries.

(International Coalition of Library Consortia, 1998b)

Why buy a dataset?

The reasons for actually embarking on the purchasing of an electronic resource will be touched upon throughout this book, but for now it is worthwhile looking at some of the generally accepted advantages of using digital over print:

- multi-access: a networked product can in theory provide multiple points of access (offices, homes, classrooms, etc.) at multiple points in time (often called '24/7', referring to the fact the resource is available 24 hours a day, 7 days a week), and to multiple simultaneous users
- speed: an electronic resource is often seen as being a lot quicker to browse or search, to extract information from, to integrate that information into other material, and to cross-search or -reference between different publications
- functionality: a dataset will allow the user to approach the publication and to analyse its content in new ways (e.g. with a dictionary one would no longer be restricted to searching under headwords)
- content: the electronic resource can contain a vast amount of information, but more importantly the material can consist of mixed media, i.e. images, video, audio, and animation, which could not be replicated in print.

Electronic collection development and traditional collection development

The question that follows on from the above is just how different is traditional collection development (the acquisition and delivery of books, journals, and so on for a library or archive) from electronic collection development (where the publications are CD-ROMs, e-journals, etc.)? If we consider the basic steps involved in traditional collection development we can outline these as follows:

- formulating a collection development policy
- establishing a budget and maintaining a record of funds
- receive notification of the resource
- evaluation of the publication
- prioritization of the publication
- purchasing (outright) or subscribing to the publication
- delivery of the publication to the reader
- monitoring usage of the publication
- subscription renewal.

It is worth considering each of these in turn and exploring the differences that may be encountered when dealing with electronic resources (note that these steps are discussed in the context of the complete life cycle of digital collection development in Chapter 4).

Formulating a collection development policy

This is standard practice in traditional collection development, but is often overlooked when it comes to building up electronic resources. This is clearly an oversight as the University of California Libraries state from the outset in their *Principles for acquiring and licensing information in digital formats*: 'Conventional collection development criteria should be paramount and should be applied consistently across formats including digital resources' (UCL, 1996, **http://sunsite.berkeley.edu/Info/principles.html**).

Too often electronic publications are purchased on a one-by-one basis, with each title being treated in isolation. The single most important message of this book is that electronic resources should be considered alongside printed resources (as indeed in some cases, such as e-journals, they must be) and that libraries should formulate an overall 'coherent' collection development policy covering all material. Such a policy should:

- outline the present collection's strengths and weaknesses (collection assessment: see Henty, 2000)
- identify the reader community that the collections are aimed at, and recognize their needs which will be met by this policy
- be made available to anyone who may be involved in purchasing decisions (the 'stakeholders', discussed in Chapter 5).

The aim is to meet the information needs of readers as quickly and efficiently as possible. The last point in the list above is extremely important. Electronic resources are often marketed at and occasionally licensed to individual subscribers, or at the very least to sub-departments. This in turn exacerbates the problem of piecemeal collection development by disparate units within institutions without any communication between them. It is almost as if the mere fact of its being an electronic resource somehow means that it could not have any effect on purchasing decisions. Such a mistake can be extremely damaging and wasteful of resources, hence the need to make the collection development policy (and subsequent decisions) available to all stakeholders. Most importantly, such a policy should be open to change and should be constantly reviewed and updated.

Establishing a budget and maintaining a record of funds

The financial systems that most institutions operate under require the establishment of a budget, and the renewal of subscriptions is often performed on an annual basis. With the exception of freely accessible internet sites, the problems faced by collection developers when it comes to establishing a budget for electronic resources and traditional (print) resources are very similar. Each year they are expected to estimate possible expenditure for the next twelve months (a topic covered in more depth in Chapter 4) and throughout the period to maintain a rolling balance of possible funds. However, there are some differences between print and digital that are worth noting now:

1   It is often very unclear as to who, within a traditional institution, should be making the decisions about the budgeting for, and purchasing of, electronic resources. Sometimes this is thrown in with traditional collection development, sometimes it is devolved down to separate departments, and so on.

2   Prices on the whole for electronic resources are often considerably higher. Even taking into account the additional advantages of using material in electronic form (noted above) it is still the case that a single product can cost thousands of pounds, and increasingly the buyer is locked into a lengthy subscription.

3   Price fluctuations in electronic resources are often completely unpredictable and well above standard inflationary rates.

Awareness of the publication

The promotion of both traditional and printed resources has many similarities. However, the notable exception to this is that the advertising of electronic resources is much more widely targeted. Publishers armed with their glossy and seductive flyers often talk to individuals and make attractive claims about the functionality of the products (most notably when it comes to delivery: see below). Although one cannot blame publishers for taking this stance (they are, after all, in the business of selling their publications), this can undoubtedly lead to problems for collection developers. It is often the case that the reader (whose enthusiasm has been whipped up by the publicity) will put pressure on the librarian to buy the title, often ignorant of the true cost implications of the product or its technical requirements.

Evaluation of the publication

There are many similarities in the processes behind evaluating print resources and electronic resources to see whether they are worth purchasing. More often than not content is the prime reason for purchasing a publication, and this can be further subdivided into its accuracy and completeness. Very often the electronic publication will be a 'reproduction' of material already in print, so the quality of the content might already be attested to. However, differences clearly lie in evaluating the usability and technical requirements of an online resource (which do not exist in the printed medium), such as the user interface, searching and response times, etc. The evaluation of electronic resources will be discussed in more detail in Chapter 4.

Prioritization of the publication

This stage requires collection developers to list all of their desiderata (their 'most wanted' titles) and prioritize them. Again the similarities between print and electronic are striking. Most people would prioritize both in terms of the current demand level, and the price. The main exception, again, would be whether the electronic resource required certain technical systems to be in place before it could be successfully delivered (i.e. prioritization would have to take into account the hidden costs behind the delivery of the digital product).

Purchasing (outright) or subscribing to the publication

Once again there is a correlation between the two media. Both electronic and print publications are sold either outright as a one-off cost, or involve a subscription (i.e. a recurrent cost – see Chapter 4 for different pricing models). The notable exception to this, however, is in the area of electronic journals and electronic books, where the subscription may be inextricably linked to that of the print version (see Chapter 3).

Delivery of the publication to the reader

It is perhaps in the area of delivery that there are the most notable differences between the electronic and print worlds. With the latter, delivery might consist of:

- cataloguing the item
- deciding on whether it is reference only, short loan, or extensive loan
- advertising the publication.

In the electronic world the decisions and problems become much more complicated and include networking, usernames and passwords, remote access, integration with existing catalogues, platform dependencies, and so on. Many of these issues are discussed in the next chapter.

Monitoring usage of the publication

Here, in terms of the two media, the reasons for monitoring usage are almost identical: namely either to save money, or to save space. If the resource involves a subscription then it is worthwhile seeing if the publication is actually being used, and if not, what the inconvenience would be if the subscription was dropped (commonly known as 'weeding' or 'de-selection'). Similarly, although physically a CD-ROM is very small (compared with a complete run of a major reference work) it does occupy digital space, i.e. storage and memory on a server. This will often require maintenance by a member of staff, so again there are possible savings to be made if the CD is taken off the server. The most notable difference between the two media is that in the electronic world one often deals with a much higher use (mainly because the products often allow for simultaneous use), and also theoretically it is much easier to keep track of user statistics, which can be generated automatically (see Chapter 5).

Subscription renewal

This is the completion of the cycle (or at least of 'a' cycle). If the product (print or electronic) is being used extensively, its continuation fits in with collection development policies, *and* there are sufficient funds, then one would probably renew the subscription. If not then the subscription may be cancelled.

It is hoped that the above analysis is a useful starting point because it allows readers of this book to feel a sense of familiarity and security. Although many of the issues we will discuss in the following chapters may be new, the underlying concept and objective – namely to build up a collection that your readers will want to use – is age-old.

Chapter summary

In this chapter we have begun to look at some of the issues surrounding the collection and management of electronic resources. In particular we have started to explore:

- the historical importance of the electronic publishing revolution
- some of the initial terminology to be used in this book, i.e. a 'dataset'
- an outline of the differences and similarities between traditional collection development and electronic collection development.

Overall this book aims to act as a guide to the purchasing and collection development of electronic resources (or datasets) but with the important assumption that this should always be viewed as being part of overall collection development. The emphasis is on those resources which involve a financial transaction. However, many of the issues in this book will be of interest to people working in legal deposit libraries or assembling freely available resources.

In the interests of space some areas have had to be dealt with in a cursory manner, and certain areas omitted altogether. In terms of looking at collection development overall this book should be used in conjunction with Liz Chapman's *Managing acquisitions* (Library Association Publishing, 2001) and Clayton and Gorman's *Managing information resources in libraries* (Library Association Publishing, 2001). For those interested in digitization, in other words the creation of your own digital resources, that area is covered in the companion to this text *Digital imaging: a practical handbook* (Lee, Library Association Publishing, 2000).

This book comes at an opportune time, indeed at a time of great change. Hanka and Fuka (2000, 280) suggested that mankind has reached a stage where we can no longer cope with the knowledge and information we possess, nor with their growth. Pity the poor librarian then who has to purchase, catalogue, and deliver this knowledge base. Moreover as David Flaxbart (2001) said:

> Libraries are approaching the time, perhaps not too distant, when the balance of our budgets will tip from hardcopy collections to leased digital information – when we pay more for access to databases and online resources than we do for putting books and journals on the shelves. This event will probably go unnoticed in most places, but that doesn't make it any less momentous. It seems like we should at least hold a small ceremony, or bury a time capsule, when the moment comes. Some of us may feel a twinge of nostalgia for simpler times, but most librarians will rightly be focused on just getting on with it.

So let us 'get on with it'. To begin to do this more thoroughly, however, we need to look at the types of electronic products available and many of the issues surrounding them.

2 What is on offer? The electronic resources landscape

Introduction

The old adage 'know your enemy' perhaps best sums up the aim of this chapter. It is important that anyone new to the area of electronic resources should be familiar with the types of products that are available and some of the main issues that surround them. In order to facilitate this, therefore, in this chapter we approach both issues. The first section deals with the major generic issues, unique in many cases, that arise when it comes to dealing with electronic resources. These range from the broad, sweeping implications of remote versus local access, to the finer issues surrounding such emerging technologies as connection files. The second section attempts to present an overall survey of the types of products currently available (e-journals, reference works, and so on).

Combined then this chapter is an attempt to *landscape* the world of the dataset. In so doing, however, it should be noted that the terms and categorizations used below are often unique to this book and would not meet with universal agreement. Furthermore, because of the vastness of the subject and the constant changes that are occurring, inevitably this summary will miss out some of the areas which certain subject specialists may deem to be important. To compensate for this readers are directed to Marian Dworaczek's exhaustive index and bibliography (**http://library. usask.ca/~dworacze/SUB_INT.HTM**), Laurence and Miller's (2000) subject guides to resources on the internet, and the Resource Guides offered by the UK's Joint Information Systems Committee (JISC) (**www.jisc.ac.uk/subject/**). Nevertheless, as an introductory guide to the issues, products, and pitfalls a collection developer will encounter, this survey will be of general use (NB the terms are further defined in the Glossary at the end of the book).

The complexity of the landscape of the dataset has recently been addressed by the United Kingdom's Distributed National Electronic Resource (DNER). In an attempt to bring together electronic resources in a seamless fashion for universities and colleges in the UK, the DNER had to confront the problem of mapping their collections so as to ascertain where there are gaps in provision. The method adopted was to look at different types of media which define in the broadest terms the landscape of the products available, and to then establish a series of working groups to look at these, in order to assist in the targeting and acquiring of new content. It is interesting therefore to note the categories that the DNER established. These were:

1   journals
2   images
3   moving images and audio
4   geospatial data
5   e-books
6   learning materials
7   discovery tools
8   research data.

This was a start. Yet as the working groups started to meet it was quickly realized that there were problems with the above categories, stemming mainly from the areas in which they overlapped. For example, a service such as JSTOR, where full back-runs of electronic journals (predominantly in the arts and social sciences) have been made available, clearly falls under the remit of the journals working group. However, JSTOR delivers facsimiles of the articles themselves and thus, in theory, it could also fall under the remit of the working group on images.

An alternative approach might be to look at the dataset in terms of its delivery of source material, i.e. whether it could be viewed as a primary, secondary or tertiary source. Again though, this leads to considerable debate and further potential confusion. The methodology adopted below, therefore, is to split the discussion into issues (interfaces versus data, remote services versus local provision, etc.) and the landscape of products and services (abstracting and indexing services, e-journals and e-books, and so on).

Issues

Although in the first chapter we explored some of the similarities between traditional collection development and electronic collection development, this should not be taken as a blanket statement that the correlation is absolute. Undoubtedly there are important differences between print and digital, and these in turn present a variety of issues that should be understood by anyone building an electronic resource collection.

Interfaces v. data

Perhaps the clearest difference between print and electronic is the fact that with the latter there is often a separation of data from the interface or delivery mechanism. This is so rare in the print world, outside of reissues or anthologies, that it is of little concern. However, when one moves to the electronic media it becomes a major issue. The scenario is simple: the data itself (the text, numerical material, images, and so on) can be devolved from the delivery platform or interface and repackaged. This generally manifests itself in a choice being offered between various suppliers, despite the fact that one is in effect buying the same data. In a sense this is a result of the adherence of publishers or data holders to cross-platform proprietary free standards, which can only be a good thing. Furthermore, choice we are always told is good, and if your institution is keen to promote a single interface then the chances of doing this are greatly increased by this separation. However, the division of the data from the interface also presents some disadvantages. First of all, too much choice can be a bad thing. Not only is the collection developer being asked to choose particular data to purchase, they may also have to evaluate a series of interfaces and suppliers.

Example

BIOSIS (**www.biosis.org.uk/**) is the main supplier of information in the life sciences, offering over 14 million citation records in electronic form under such popular titles as *Biological Abstracts* and *Zoological Records*. Yet the information is held in such a form that it is possible to deliver it via a variety of commercial interfaces, access routes, or, as they are more commonly known, 'service providers'. The BIOSIS data, for example, can be provided by Dialog/Data-Star (**www.dialog.com/**), Elsevier Science (**www.elsevier.nl/** or **www.elsevier.com/**), the Deutsches Institut für Medizinische Dokumentation und Information (**www.dimdi.de/**), ISI (**www.isinet.com/isi/**), Ovid (**www.ovid.com/**), and its sister company SilverPlatter (**www.silverplatter.com/**), to name but a few. When buying BIOSIS, then, collection developers not only have to decide that this is the data the users want, but they also have to choose between six or more suppliers.

A similar example to the above is the US National Library of Medicine's MEDLINE. Once again the data provided can be purchased through a variety of deals and service providers. This in turn points to a further problem associated with this apparent liberty of choice. Because of MEDLINE's understandable popularity and importance, it is often one of the most used datasets on the network of any institution that covers the medical sciences. Therefore, if the licence for the product is based on limited use, and MEDLINE is only one of a series of products bundled together, then it is important to monitor its usage so that it does not swamp access to other datasets. The collection developer has to be aware of all the potential sources of the various datasets made available, but more importantly he or she will want to be certain that the same package is not being needlessly paid for more than once.

Remote *v.* local

The internet has changed the concept of 'place' in relation to both collections and collectors. In the electronic world, it has become less important WHERE a document resides and more important to have reliable, well organized (and presented) access to it. We want to know who produced it, who identified it as valuable, and who selected it for our use, but that person does not have to sit at the desk next to us. We no longer need to 'own' a physical manifestation of the information in our private institutional domain, but we must provide the appropriate technological and organizational infrastructure to access it reliably.

(Baldwin and Mitchell, *Untangling the Web Conference*, 1996,
www.library.ucsb.edu/untangle/baldwin.html)

The location of the point of service for the datasets can be crucial. Before the widespread uptake of the web most products came as CD-ROMs or on magnetic tape. The onus then was on the local institution to either present these as networked resources (i.e. mounting them on their local server) or as standalone packages (in the case of CD-ROMs) which could then be borrowed and used on individual machines.

There were (and still are) many problems with this sort of provision. First and foremost there are costs at the local end, not just for the technology itself (i.e. the server, network backbone, and client machines) but also for the staff needed to mount the dataset, check that it really is networkable, and maintain it and any updates issued as part of the subscription. In the case of standalone products the costs are still there in the form of configuring individual machines, and the benefits are greatly reduced as only one person can access the product at a time. Moreover, the design of many of these products leaves a lot to be desired. The majority require the dataset to be run on a Windows operating system, thus disenfranchizing other platform users (such as UNIX or Macintosh).

At the same time, although the products are marketed as being suitable for networking, they still often require mapping to local hard drives or a place to write information back to (which can be technically difficult on open-access machines and secure servers). Generally, though, this is a problem of the interface or searching software – not the data. The products are also designed to be used individually (even on a network), i.e. the possibility of cross-searching is generally nonexistent. The most obvious exceptions to this are SilverPlatter products (or SP compliant datasets) which can be run together on a unique server, thus allowing cross-searching and also cross-platform use by the WebSPIRS interface.

Multimedia titles that are run locally may also cause problems, requiring higher specification client machines, a good local area network, and a variety of third-party players.

As we will discover when we look at licensing in Chapter 4, publishers often impose certain access restrictions, such as a limit on the number of simultaneous users, which will also require some technical expertise at the local level. All these present hidden costs which must be considered in the original decision to purchase.

Remote access, in theory, overcomes many of these problems. Although this has been around for some time and interfaces and communication protocols used have differed in the past, most products now are available via the single interface of the world wide web. At a stroke then the burden on the local institution is greatly reduced by using web access to remote services. No longer do you have to maintain a local server, you simply need to list the URL of the remote site. However, some of the problems listed above still remain. The local institution will sometimes have to manage the authorization of users (e.g. by maintaining lists of legitimate names – see below), or buy into the publisher's own authentication system and locally administer usernames and passwords.

The web is, of course, cross-platform, thus opening the resource up to all users (though it is often clear that publishers rarely test their products fully on a wide range of operating systems and platforms). In most cases the product will simply use standard web protocols, and can be accessed by mainstream browsers with no configuration, but sometimes it will require the downloading and installation of additional software such as plug-ins. Again this may present problems at the local end. Speed of access may also be a problem with remote access, as perhaps will charges occasionally levied for internet traffic.

Web delivery does present an interesting difficulty in defining the scope of a publication. Increasingly, for example, online publications make use of links to other external sites. Unsuspecting users therefore can quickly find themselves using information from another completely different site without fully realizing this. This may not cause too many problems, but if a user wishes to reuse material they may struggle to find out where they can contact the rights owner.

Example 1

The electronic *Encyclopaedia Britannica* (*EB*) originally came out as a CD-ROM product. This was successfully marketed to individuals (indeed sales stalls even appeared in supermarkets and high-street shops), but there were inherent problems. First, it was in fact a two-CD product, which required swapping between the discs. Second, the CDs were limited to the Windows platform only, and networking them was never that easy. When *EB* migrated to the web (**www.eb.com**) many of these problems evaporated. Suddenly it was cross-platform, it did not require disc-swapping, and more importantly it could utilize hyperlinks to external sites. However, the links to external sites are often unsatisfactory, as the content may not be up to the standard of the *EB* (though there is some attempt to grade them).

Example 2

The *Oxford English dictionary* was one of the ground-breaking electronic publications of the 1990s. Suddenly, the potential the new digital medium had to offer was obvious. All the volumes could now fit on a single CD, were completely searchable and, of course, were cross-referenced. More importantly the user was no longer limited to looking up headwords. The user could search for occurrences of a word within definitions, or even perform complex searches such as 'all words that came into popular usage since 1980'. However, as with most CDs the product was limited to the Windows platform, but networking it was relatively easy. When the dictionary moved to the web (**http://dictionary.oed.com/**) it became available via simple internet access. Yet, as is often the case with publications that started life on CD and then moved to the internet, the interface and functionality available to the users was suddenly very limited. The CD allowed for much more advanced search queries that could not be accommodated in the web version.

Remote access mirrors

Another issue that is tangential to remote and local access is that of 'mirrors'. In short these are copies (i.e. reflections) of the original source item that the user wishes to look at. For example, colleges in the United Kingdom can access the UK mirror service (**www.mirror.ac.uk**), which collects together complete sites or individual pieces of software which it feels will be of interest to its constituents. The aim is to allow people in the UK quicker access to these services (as they now only have to use the national network), and possibly this may have cost implications limiting charges imposed on international traffic.

The main issue that surrounds mirrors, though, is that of currency. How up to date is the copy that you are accessing? In the case of the above service the collections are updated daily, and automatically, but with some sites this may not always be the case. Users need to be aware of exactly what they are searching. Furthermore, mirror sites do pose problems of maintaining accurate links to the resources. If the mirror service was to cease the user would then have to track down all the addresses of the individual services of which it stored copies.

Umbrella products and bundled deals

Although 'umbrella products' should not be considered a major problem, they are worth noting in this survey of the issues surrounding electronic resources. A simple example is a series of individual products collected together under a single title (hence the term 'umbrella'), such as the Research Libraries Group service – EUREKA (**http://eureka.rlg.org/**). This comprises nearly 20 titles such as the *Bibliography of the history of art*, the *English short title catalogue*, and so on). There are two problems that may arise from this. First, users should be aware that there are various 'subtitles' available, otherwise they may overlook valuable resources. The second problem is for collection developers themselves, in that they need to keep accurate records of all these 'subtitles' which are bundled together under a single term, in order to avoid duplicate subscriptions.

With e-journals and e-books this is a particularly acute problem. As we will see later, deals that are negotiated will generally include the complete list of titles from a particular publisher. Ideally here one would wish to select subgroups if possible (also known as 'disaggregation'), but more often than not such a level of selection is not allowed.

Push/pull technology

To add to the overall uncertainty of where the data is held, there is also the problem of who is responsible for disseminating the information. With the web the onus is on the user to actually go to a site to see if it has been updated recently. With e-mail, messages are sent directly to the user's inbox (although the user does, of course, have to open the e-mail to read it). This is a good analogy to help explain the concept of 'push/pull' technology. With push technology, as with e-mail, the information is sent and received with minimal effort on the user's part. With pull technology, as with the web, the users must retrieve the information themselves.

This manifests itself most noticeably in the electronic resources arena with current awareness systems (CAS). This is a generic term for systems that allow users to be kept up to date with news about their subject area, emerging technologies, and so on. A good example of such a system is an alerting service. Here, through some automatic process, the user is 'alerted' to new additions to datasets of particular interest. Without such dataset updates users would have to rely on pull technology: that is to say they would actually have to go to the dataset and redo their searches. With an alerting service they could be automatically notified of any updates.

Example

The British Library Electronic Table of Contents (ETOC) has been made available in the United Kingdom via the ZETOC service (Z39.50 ETOC). This allows users to search the contents of thousands of journals and conference proceedings, and set up a basic alerting service. Having selected a list of up to 50 journal titles, whenever a new issue of any of these is added to the dataset the user is automatically notified via e-mail of the table of contents.

Alerting services are just one useful instance of push technology, but there are many other services that, combined or used separately, would be classed as a current awareness system. It should be noted, however, that some elements that would go towards making up a current awareness system are sold as separate products, and do not come as a free add-on as with the ZETOC alerting service noted above. ISI's Current Contents Connect (CCC) is a good example of this, as it includes a profile-based alerting service that gives users the ability to create and manage a set number of alerts using ISI's Current Contents data. The results are then e-mailed to the user once a week. However, CCC is clearly marketed and sold as a distinct product that collection managers would have to evaluate and purchase from new, i.e. it is not a free utility added on to another service. In this sense then CCC is a good example of an area that crosses over from the discussion of emerging technologies to that of the types of products available. In other words, some features, utilities, and technologies have to be purchased in the same way an entire product is.

Common also to both ZETOC and CCC is the concept of 'profiles'. In this a user can set up a personalized user space for themselves allowing for the creation of links to specific journal titles, the ability to retain searches for future sessions, and so on. For such profiles to be successful, though, they need to be associated with an individual (or at least an identifiable group) so that no-one else can alter the settings in the profile. The way that an individual is identified in the world of electronic resources is often termed 'authentication'.

Authentication

Authentication is a means by which a publisher or supplier (and here the supplier could be the local institution) can discriminate between legitimate users and those not allowed access to the product. This is opposite to the idea of open access, where no restrictions apply. Two common forms of authentication are discussed below.

Username and password

Here the individual is prompted to enter a username and password prior to accessing the resource. The username and password may be generic for the institution or linked to one or more specific individuals – sometimes one username and password will be shared by several people (e.g. an entire department). Usernames and passwords do not necessarily have to be the traditional character string, and sometimes may utilize barcodes (as used on identity cards).

The advantage of this system is that it can identify use by a particular individual or group of individuals. This can be useful for tracking use (possibly just for monitoring purposes, but also for charging), for building profiles (users can save their searches and return to them in the future), but above all (from the supplier's point of view) for penalizing misuse. That is to say, should a username be identified as being the main per-petrator of excessive downloads or copyright infringements then it can be suspended relatively easily.

There are also disadvantages. Usernames are very easy to pass on, and such misuse may only be traced by an excessive number of searches under the same username from different geographical locations (in a short space of time). But the onus here would be on the supplier to check for such occurrences. The system also places a heavy administrative burden on the person (usually the librarian) charged with issuing and updating usernames and passwords, or dealing with forgotten passwords. Users may find it troublesome to remember a series of different usernames and passwords, each tied to an individual service. To overcome this latter problem there are systems such as ATHENS, whereby each user in the UK academic sector is issued with a single username and password, and publishers and suppliers are encouraged to use this single point of authentication.

IP Authentication

Internet protocol authentication is based on a form of identification using internet standards (the username and password solution can relate to non-internet-based products). This usually means that the supplier of the dataset checks that the user is legitimate according to the IP address, i.e.

the code that identifies the user's computer to the rest of the internet. Every machine using the internet has a specific IP address in the form of a series of four numbers separated by points, e.g. 123.4.56.78. You can look on this as being similar to a telephone number. From left to right the numbers gradually get more specific to the machine, so in the above example '123.4.56' may be identifying the institution, its type, the department within the institution and so on, whilst '78' could be the individual machine. This unique number therefore can be a handy way of authenticating use. The supplier of the remote dataset maintains a list of all IP numbers of legitimate machines: when the user is trying to access the dataset the IP address of the client machine is automatically checked against the supplier's own list. If the numbers tally then access is granted.

More commonly a subscription is taken out by a whole institution rather than an individual (or group of individuals), so it is easier for the supplier to be given, and to maintain, a list of the root IP addresses (rather than every number for each machine), e.g. '123.4.56.x' (with 'x' implying any number). A subscription may also be based on the domain name of the machine. This is a character-based identifier rather than numerical and thus more recognizable to the user, e.g. 'gov.uk', 'ox.ac.uk' or 'wvu.edu' (the domain name often appears in URLs for the websites of that institution). This means of authentication tells the supplier that you want to allow access to the dataset from all machines within, for example, the 'gov.uk' domain. This is an extremely good way of getting large amounts of users authenticated very quickly (e.g. to allow access to a dataset by all users in the US and Canadian higher education sector one would simply have to use the domain name '.edu').

As with the username and password system there are advantages and disadvantages to the IP authentication system. The main plus is the ease by which it can be set up and maintained by both supplier and client (usually by an administrator). The relevant information the supplier needs is simply a list of root IP numbers or, even easier, a domain name. The administrative burden increases considerably, however, if one has to specify individual IP addresses, and this in turn means only specific machines may be used. Another advantage is, of course, that IP authentication involves no intervention by the user. The process is performed automatically (once it has been set up), and thus users avoid the problems of mistyping or forgetting passwords.

The disadvantages to IP authentication come in two major areas. First, one has no control over who is accessing the material, only where they are accessing it from (physically or virtually). Although we have noted that passwords can be traded, it is still possible to trace misuse of the system to a particular individual (or more correctly to a particular username). In IP authentication one can often only trace misuse to the machine the perpetrator was sitting at, not the individual's identity (unless access to the machine is somehow monitored). This can present problems when one has open access to computers, such as in a public library.

The second major concern surrounding IP authentication is that it does not easily allow for remote use – that is to say, users who wish to access the dataset when they are away from the host institution. Over the past couple of years the proliferation of free or relatively cheap internet service providers (ISPs) has meant that many users look to the likes of AOL or FreeServe as their first port of call for internet access. There is nothing wrong in this, of course, but as soon as users connect to these ISPs they are allocated an IP number specific to that company. The user will then be unable to access a dataset that is using IP authentication (unless the ISP has taken out a subscription to the service, and this is very unlikely).

Example

A worker at a publishing company regularly accesses the online *Oxford English dictionary* site, being able to do so because the company has taken out a subscription. However, during a visit abroad she wishes to look at the *OED* again. She connects to the internet via the local branch of her domestic ISP. Because she is now identified on the internet (by her IP number) differently from when she was at work, she is prohibited from accessing the dictionary. One option in this case is to dial in to the firm's system and be allocated an IP number by them. However, this incurs the cost of an international telephone call.

Alternatively, if a VPN client has previously been installed (see below) on the machine she will be using when abroad, she can access the internet using any local ISP, launch the VPN client, and access her employer's VPN server. She is then assigned an IP number for the company itself, thus allowing her to access the *OED*.

A possible solution is the gradual appearance of virtual private networks (VPNs). With a VPN the client can link directly into a network, regardless of what ISP or LAN (local area network) is being used. Users are assigned an IP number for their institution via the VPN server, thus allowing them to use all the datasets restricted by IP authentication.

It has been discovered that the use of cacheing (especially if using a system open to many differing institutions) and proxies can disrupt IP authentication. Thus a user, even if located within an institution that has subscribed to a dataset, may have to turn off the web browser proxies or ask for the site to be exempted from the cache in order to gain access. Similarly cookies can cause a problem as users often rely on them to store their authentication details. If the cookies are lost, perhaps as a result of a system upgrade, then a major administrative exercise may have to be initiated.

The choice of authentication system need not be a straightforward decision between either the password authentication model *or* some form of IP checking. Some suppliers employ both systems, thus performing double authentication checks: i.e. they first of all see that the machine is part of the subscribing institution via IP authentication and then ask for a username and password. This validation system is often seen as providing much greater security. Other suppliers offer a choice between the two, so that if, say, IP authentication fails, the user can still gain access via a prearranged username and password. This scenario is often considered very desirable as it caters for both local and remote use by legitimate users. Finally, some products utilize such things as public keys, X.509 certificates, and tokens, which attempt to streamline the authentication procedure from one dataset to another. These terms may be unfamiliar to many, and would require a lengthy explanation to communicate their full meaning. However, simply put, they allow for checking validity of use by agreed mechanisms. The keys and certificates are often referred to as digital signatures.

If we were to define authentication in its widest possible sense we might also say that it is linked to any access restriction dictated by the licence agreement. For example, some suppliers place restrictions on simultaneous access (e.g. only five people at any given time can use the product), or the number of hours the dataset can be used per month by the institution. Again this implies that some form of system must be in place to check that the licence has not been infringed. Although, strictly speaking, users are not being authenticated in the sense that there is a check as to whether they should or should not be using it, they are being assessed as to whether they should be using the product at that particular time. The range of such licensing agreements will be discussed at length in Chapter 4.

Connection files, special features, and downloading results

The usability and special features offered by services will come up again when we look at evaluating a product in Chapter 4, but for now it is worth looking briefly at some additional features that are on offer. These tend to appear at three stages:

- during the initial connection to the dataset
- whilst actually searching or browsing the dataset
- when managing and downloading the results.

We have already looked at the initial connection to the dataset under authentication, whereby an intermediate system checks the legitimacy of the user (via username and password, IP authentication, or both), and either allows them to continue or prohibits further use. We must also consider utilities that allow users to connect directly to a dataset from a third-party piece of software. Here the 'connection file' is the bridging piece of software that brings the two together.

Example

There is already an established interest amongst researchers in the use of reference managing tools. ISI ResearchSoft's EndNote product is a typical example, allowing the user to collect together references, sort and output them in a variety of styles, and link them directly to their word processor. However, in the past interfacing these products with the online abstracting and indexing services (see below) has often been problematic. In many cases the user is required to save results in a predefined format, copy them to disk or have them e-mailed to a personal account, and then somehow import them into the bibliographic software. Needless to say this is not ideal (nor is it trouble-free). 'Connection files' specifically written to connect to individual catalogues or services have recently emerged. These allow users to open up their bibliographic software package, link directly to the services of their choice (from within the software), search the remote service (albeit using a limited interface) and download the results directly back into their library of references.

At the most extreme this might involve an elaborate setup that would allow a user to search across a series of disparate datasets from a single source, meaning that the products could be housed locally or remotely, and in theory may be from different suppliers. Although no bibliographic software at the moment can offer such a facility, gateways are emerging that can assist in this. More often than not these use the Z39.50 protocol, which in simple terms is a standard way of describing searches and results to allow cross-communication between suppliers. In other words, a user could enter a search term into a single interface and this then would be sent to all services that are Z39.50 compliant, returning the hits from these disparate sources back to the single interface. Theoretically, therefore, this search could be launched from a third-party piece of software through a connection file (or series of files).

We should also include a brief mention of the types of add-ons or utilities many services provide to help users manage their results. A simple example of this is the choice between a quick search and an advanced search (the latter providing the user with much more control over the query syntax). Similarly, once the results are returned how can the user easily manage these? We have already noted that some services allow the results to be e-mailed to the user or to be saved to disk, and many services also allow users to describe the desired complexity of their results. When looking at an abstracting and indexing service, for example, some users may be interested in receiving only brief bibliographic details, whereas others may want to see the record in full. More importantly a search may yield 50 reasonably relevant results, out of which only 20 are specifically useful to the researcher: many services allow the user to select individual records. To summarize the above, then, a service may allow you to:

- mark results for further study
- expand results
- view abstracts
- link to holdings or other services
- create user profiles for future use.

Linkage services

The term 'linkage service' can mean one of three things in the digital world:

1   A service, usually commercially driven, that seeks out sites of relevance to a firm's target area and suggests that the remote site links directly to the institution or company's site (i.e. a reciprocal link). This helps to build up a matrix of links to the local site and thus increase its market potential.

2   Linking between an index and more substantial amounts of data (much more relevant to the focus of this book). Ostensibly this derives from the software market where linking between such things as database records is common, but for the purposes outlined here, it is common for a table of contents, say, to link directly to the full text of the book or article. Understandably, therefore, the collection developer will most often encounter the term 'linkage service' when dealing with e-journals.

3   Linking from within articles (usually) to other articles (an extension of

the second example). In other words, there is the availability of automatic cross-referencing.

Example

The ISI Web of Science Service is an extensive list of the contents of several thousand journals, the main databases being the *Science Citation Index*, the *Social Sciences Citation Index*, and the *Arts & Humanities Citation Index*. The typical user will type in a search term and retrieve a series of bibliographic records. In the past users would then locate the book or article in their or another library and consult the physical item itself. However, now that many journals are available online, the search results can be linked to the online article itself. The ISI linkage service allows users whose institution has paid all the appropriate subscriptions to follow their search results directly to the online holdings of the Academic Press, American Institute of Physics, American Physical Society, Blackwell Science, Catchword, Karger, Kluwer Academic Press, ScienceDirect, and so on.

Linkage services will be discussed in more detail in Chapter 3.

Archiving and long-term access

The archiving and maintained long-term access to any digital product is surrounded by many problems and issues (see Lee, 2000), but particular concerns are presented for collection developers. Print material, assuming it is on reasonable paper, will remain intact for decades or even centuries. Therefore the one-off payment when one buys a monograph will generally mean that your readers in the future will have access to that publication (barring theft, destruction, or weeding). However, once one moves into the electronic world the preservation of material, and consequently the assured future access to it, becomes an extremely thorny issue. As the ICOLC states:

It is critical to libraries and the constituents they serve that permanent archival access to information be available, especially if that information exists only in electronic form. Libraries cannot rely solely on external providers to be their archival source. Therefore, agreements to procure e-information must include provisions to purchase and not just to lease or provide temporary access.

(International Coalition of Library Consortia, 1998b)

Let us take a CD-ROM purchase as an example. For the present, it may be relatively easy to network such a product and provide access to it, and to keep the original master CD itself in a safe location (i.e. if the licence permits it the data could be copied to a server, and then the physical disk stored in a fire safe, or indeed several copies could be dispersed in different locations). However, what happens when the technology the CD relies on becomes obsolete? It is not hard to envisage a future where CD-ROM readers are only found in museums, and more importantly the operating system (e.g. Windows or Mac OS) required to run the searching software for the CD is no longer available. How then does the librarian attempt to maintain continued access to the resource (a particular issue for legal deposit libraries)? The general answers to this would be to:

1   maintain a collection of all the hardware needed to run the CD
2   create software packages that emulate the original operating systems
3   somehow extract the data held in the publication and migrate it into new searching software.

Yet none of the above could be argued to be a realistic option for each library to undertake. The sheer costs involved, and the technical knowledge required, could not be covered by all institutions. In this sense then one can only hope that a national solution (along the lines of the legal deposit libraries, such as the Library of Congress or the British Library) will be found, so that at least one copy of the publication is still usable in the future.

When it comes to the subscription model, whereby a library pays a regular amount of money to a remote supplier (e.g. for access to an electronic journal), the problem is a different one. Here it is up to the vendor (in theory) to maintain access to the product, and one would hope that most publishers have built in a migration strategy into their future plans. Yet there is still a major problem for the library. If the institution finds that for financial reasons it will have to cut its subscription, it is possible that it will be prohibited from accessing any part of the product (though Atherton, 2001, noted that 77% of e-journal publishers do allow access to archives after cancellation, but only for a maximum of five years). For example, let us suppose a library has been paying an annual subscription to a publisher to access its electronic journals online, and continues to do so for five years. In the sixth year budget cuts result in the cancellation of the subscription. This may mean in practice that not only the latest issues of the journal but also the five-year back-run are no longer available. If this had been a subscription to a print run then at least the old copies would still have been on the shelves.

Yet all is not lost. Many publishers are looking to a model (when it comes to journals) of only charging for access to the most recent issues and making back-runs freely available (particularly in the sciences, where the currency of the information is most prized). Furthermore, some licences allow subscribers to have 'permanent' access to the issues paid for (indeed they may even be sent the data itself). This, for example, was the model sought by the National Electronic Site Licence Initiative (NESLI), which set up many national deals for e-journals in the United Kingdom.

User interface

Some preliminary issues surrounding the interface the user encounters were touched on earlier, and they will also be looked at when we come to discussing how a dataset might be delivered (see Chapter 5). In general, though, there are two interfaces the collection manager will need to consider when trying to maximize the benefit to users:

1   The interface provided by the supplier. More often than not the individual institution will have little control over this, and one's only option would be to provide feedback directly to the supplier. Nevertheless, the look and feel of a service, and the facilities it offers, will

be taken into account when considering whether to buy or subscribe to a product.

2   The interface provided by the local institution to their users. This is certainly more in the control of the institution, and serious thought should be given to its design and structure, as these will directly affect how the products it connects to are used. A lengthier discussion of this is outlined in Chapter 5.

The landscape

Having looked at some of the major technical issues surrounding electronic resources, or more importantly some of the factors that make them different from print-based resources, we should now turn our attention to the range of products that are available. It is not feasible, of course, to discuss every individual product that is on sale as such a list would run to volumes – and nor would this be a particularly helpful exercise or one appropriate to our present discussion. As mentioned in the introduction, the main aim of this book is to present collection managers, new to the field of electronic resources, with an overview of the problems and products they will encounter. The following description of the landscape is an introductory overview, using a series of categories under which products could be reasonably defined. As previously noted, these categories will not meet with universal agreement, and any attempt at taxonomy will always lead to prolonged debate. Furthermore the list below is not comprehensive and certain areas unique to individual subject areas have not been included.

Abstracting and indexing services, and other bibliographic sources (OPACs, citation indexes, TOCs, etc.)

The ability of the computer to store data in the form of records, and allow quick searching of these, has long been recognized. Therefore it is understandable that one of the most important electronic reference tools used in libraries worldwide (and probably the oldest) is the online catalogue. Online public access catalogues (or OPACs) allow readers to search or browse the catalogue and to quickly locate books and journals. This, however, is also a commodity. The sheer intellectual exercise that goes into cataloguing material is of value, and therefore it is not surprising that some of the major research libraries offer their catalogues to others (in the main these are free, but in the not-too-distant past these were also available for purchase – usually on CD-ROM). The underlying system used by the library will differ from institution to institution, but in most cases OPACs provide a web interface (though some still only allow for Telnet or 'terminal' accesses), quick hyperlinked cross-searching, and downloading of results.

These are not the only major bibliographic resources on offer. Abstracting and indexing services (A&I services) are numerous, with some very big services already available (such as those offered by ISI, Dialog and OCLC). Generally these offer the user the ability to search vast collections of table of content (TOC) data from books and serials, and in some cases (such as the British Library's Electronic Table of Contents) conference proceedings. The benefit of these large services is that they cover many subjects and thus facilitate a multidisciplinary approach.

In most cases the user will be presented with a simple search or advanced search option (the latter utilizing Boolean operators AND, OR and NOT, for example) which will return a series of 'hits', in this case abbreviated bibliographic references containing the user's search terms. From there the user will usually be allowed to expand each reference, mark or select the record for later use, and in some cases be allowed to link to an abstract, or the institution's OPAC.

The ISI's citation indexes offer a development of the above. Not only can these be viewed as an A&I service (i.e. they allow you to search TOCs and indexes), they also allow for searching citations. This provides two benefits. First, one can quickly check the 'impact factor' of an article or book, by seeing how often it is cited elsewhere. Second, when looking at a reference one can quickly see what other works are cited in it, allowing for an instant snapshot of the tone and coverage of the article, and at the same time providing routes for further research.

In addition, there are more 'subject specific' lists. SocioFile is a g[?] example of this. Here the TOCs are collected with a certain series of disciplines in mind (i.e. the social sciences). The very name of the product will make it attractive to those specific users, and it will often appear high in their list of most-used datasets. To this we could add Biological Abstracts, MEDLINE, and the International Medieval Bibliography – all of which are prime examples of TOC services aimed at a specific set of subject disciplines. Nevertheless, names of products can be misleading. Not only do we have the problem where the title itself gives very little away to the user as to the product's full contents, but researchers in other areas may be deterred from using the resource. SocioFile, for example, would be of interest to some scholars in the humanities (such as economic history), and ISI's Web of Science is clearly of interest to all subject areas as the indices cover the arts, social sciences, and pure sciences. In most cases the way to tackle this is a well-designed interface at the local institution level, as well as comprehensive and targeted user training (see Chapter 5).

Numerical collections and textbases

These are the collections that contain vast amounts of primary source material or research data (as opposed to simply listing the contents of journals or monographs). Numerical collections contain such things as official statistics and economic returns, scientific and mathematical research results, and so on. These may be part of an established print series already available to researchers, or could be direct 'live' feeds from large research projects and institutions (such as meteorological data collected on a daily basis).

Example

EIU (Economist Intelligence Unit) Country Data covers over 100 countries, providing numerical data on all the nations and regions listed. The EIU calculates aggregate lists and presents them to the user. All of the countries listed, as well as additional regions, come with an EIU country outlook, which is a short summary on the economic status of the area. However, the bulk of the information provided is numerical.

A textbase on the other hand is a large collection of electronic texts that are available for searching. The immediate difficulty arises in trying to distinguish a textbase, using this definition, from an electronic journal or electronic book. With textbases we tend to be dealing with anthologies, usually (but not always) based in the humanities, as opposed to a series (as in e-journals) or individual texts (with e-books). A textbase should also present all the text as being fully searchable (i.e. not simply facsimiles of pages linked to searchable bibliographic data). Such a definition may not satisfy everyone but for the purposes of this discussion it will suffice.

One manifestation of the textbase that is common to all subjects is the reference work – the encyclopaedia or dictionary. Another is the large corpus of material, fully searchable, covering complete genres or the entire works of an author. As with many products these are delivered on CD-ROM, on magnetic tape, via the web, or in some cases by all three methods. The complexity of the searching often relies on the level of mark-up introduced by the publisher – mark-up being the way individual elements of the text are described (e.g. parts of speech, paragraphs, chapters, etc.).

Example

During the 1990s Chadwyck-Healey Ltd were the main pioneers in this area, although others such as Brepols should be noted. In that period Chadwyck-Healey issued such titles as the *Patrologia Latina* (a large series of patristic texts), and more importantly their Literature On-Line service (which brought together some of their CD-ROM products and added many new titles). This was web-based and allowed readers to search and browse most of the works of British and American literature (and in effect have access to an enormous downloadable library). The site is available via an annual subscription.

E-journals

E-journals are simply electronic representations of a journal. In most cases these replicate the printed version of the journal exactly, occasionally including additional information (such as interactive graphs or external links), but in some cases there is no parallel print source and the journal was 'born digital'. However, behind this simple definition lies a complicated scenario involving aggregators, publishers, new licensing deals, and so on. Reflecting this, and the fact that e-journals have risen in importance over the last few years, they are treated in more detail in the following chapter.

E-books

An e-book is an electronic representation of a book, usually a parallel publication of a print copy, but occasionally, like the journal, it has been born digital. Such products as the Grove *Dictionaries* (art, opera, and music) are in theory e-books, as they represent in electronic form the contents of those in print. Yet the term 'e-book' has taken on a meaning of its own, tending really to focus on single books (usually textbooks but occasionally fiction), marketed often for use in a third party browser (or reader) or on a specialized piece of hardware. For this reason in this book we make a distinction between e-books and reference books, placing the latter under the category noted above of 'textbases'. Again, because of the complexities surrounding this area, its popularity at the moment (in terms of how much concern e-books are causing collection managers), and the similarities with e-journals, further discussion of these products is deferred to the next chapter.

Multimedia products

Certain electronic resources could be classified as multimedia publications. Looking at the strictest definition of multimedia as a product that combines two or more of the main media types – text, images, audio, video, animation – then it is clear that many products come under this heading (e.g. when they combine text and facsimile images of pages). In the majority of cases this will not cause any problems to the collection manager. However, if the product includes audio and/or video there may be problems for both the person attempting to network the product (notoriously difficult unless it can be delivered via web browser) and the librarian attempting to control the environment where the product will be used (it may be necessary to configure the client machine so that it can play both the sound and the video without disturbing other readers). Also, if the product requires special plug-ins to be used, a problem can arise when machines are overloaded with excessive numbers of such 'utilities'; moreover it may be difficult to exert control over the client machine (i.e. it may be in the reader's home where necessary hardware or software may not be available).

Yet multimedia products can be easy to use, and above all extremely beneficial to the end-user. A lot of institutions buy into (or indeed create their own) image databases, for example. A prime illustration of this is the AMICO dataset (available via the EUREKA service), consisting of thousands of images of fine art. Another specific (and almost unique in its own right) example of a multimedia product is that of the digital map collection. Here maps are delivered as images for online manipulation, or for downloading to third-party software.

Example

The DigiMap service in the UK is one of the leading map datasets. Here the user can 'make maps' using five resources provided by the country's Ordinance Survey institution. The service allows users to analyse maps online (i.e. zooming in to different scales), or download them for printing or for use in GIS (geographic information systems) software.

News services

Many newspapers have a website detailing that day's news, some offering articles stretching back a few weeks or longer. These pages are clearly very useful to businesses and researchers (and will probably form part of any current awareness system), and moreover they are generally free. However, what is also of interest are the longer back-runs of newspapers, and the proliferation of news services or news feeds. The newspaper archive is really just an extension of the textbase noted above (especially when one looks at the historical archives such as Chadwyck-Healey's *Times* products). A subscription allows the user to search the text of newspapers going back ten to twenty years, or even centuries. Bringing together some of the points raised earlier in this chapter, such collections present the problems associated with 'umbrella products', that is to say you will often subscribe to a single service such as Dialog, Reuters, or LEXIS–NEXIS and be offered hundreds of titles. The collection developer will need to be aware of which ones are supplied, how far back the archives go, and whether they are the full text of the papers or just simply abstracts. Second, there is the problem of the data being separate from a single supplier. As we have just observed, Dialog, Reuters, and LEXIS–NEXIS are but three of many suppliers of newspaper archives, all with very similar holdings. The problem, therefore, is to keep track of the papers one wishes to make available to readers and the contents offered by the various suppliers.

Information, and more importantly *up-to-date* information, is an extremely valuable commodity. Another aspect, therefore, is the presentation of comprehensive news as quickly as possible (e.g. political events, share prices, and so on). Collection developers may therefore wish to subscribe to a news feed. Very often this will employ a mixture of pull and push technology. Sometimes, as with Reuters Business Briefing, the user will still need to access the service to search for new information. Other products, such as those made available by the BBC, CNN, and Reuters itself, push news items out to the user (occasionally called rolling news services). For an example of an 'intelligent' news service see the AdaptiveInfo service (**www.adaptiveinfo.com/**) and their demonstration of a personalized version of the *Los Angeles Times* (**www.adaptiveinfo. com/Products/demonstration.asp**).

Conclusion

At the beginning of this chapter we noted an initiative within the United Kingdom by the DNER to try to map out 'areas of content' or the landscape of the electronic resource. In their exercise they chose to define their categories as: journals, images, moving images and audio, geospatial data, e-books, learning materials, discovery tools, and research data. For the purposes of this chapter we have split the discussion further into current issues and technologies (i.e. the separation of data from a single supplier, the idea of remote versus local access, mirroring services, umbrella products, push/pull technology, authentication, connection files, managing results, linkage services, and archiving) and the types of content on offer (A&I services, numerical collections, textbases, e-journals and e-books, and multimedia products). It is clear that any attempt to define the landscape of the dataset will be beset by all kinds of problems. How can you hope to define something so large and constantly changing? Nevertheless, with this overview of the types of products and issues the collection manager will encounter we have at least made a start.

Chapter summary

In this chapter we have covered the following points:

- the main issues that arise with electronic resources, many of which are unique to this area of collection development
- the types of products that are available for purchase or subscription (i.e. the landscape of the dataset).

In the next chapter we will continue this discussion by focusing in particular on two areas of growing interest and concern to collection developers: the electronic journal and the electronic book.

3

E-books and e-journals

Introduction

In Chapter 2 we outlined some of the issues that surround electronic resources which differentiate them from print publications. Furthermore we presented a general map of the range of products one might encounter with a few examples where appropriate. Here we focus on two of these types of product, e-books and e-journals. There are obviously clear differences in the issues these present to the collection developer (notably e-books, for example, which can be marketed to individuals and may require special devices to read them, as we shall see), but there are clearly some strong similarities. Points to note include:

1. E-journals and e-books are extremely topical at the moment
2. E-journals command particular attention as on average a collection developer in a standard academic library spends about 90% of the acquisition budget on serials
3. There are a range of suppliers (many of them small companies with uncertain futures), deals, licensing models, and so on, for both products
4. Collection developers are trying to build models to cope with both e-journals and e-books
5. The number of individual titles that can be purchased is much larger than those in other areas (e.g. multimedia collections, statistical data-sets, and so on), and therefore it is more common to see bulk deals (bundles or umbrella products)

6 Bulk deals are often the complete list of journals or books of a publisher or a series of publishers; this can cause notable problems (especially with books) where very few institutions would want to buy such a selection

7 The separation of data from a single supplier is extremely noticeable with these products – publishers of both journals and books are marketing their content via a variety of suppliers at the same time

8 Aggregators or intermediaries are very common in both markets, acting as middle points between the consumer and the publisher (as they traditionally have in the purchases of serials and monographs)

9 Most e-books and e-journals are delivered in a proprietary standard (i.e. the publishers' own method or, more commonly, Adobe's PDF)

10 Linkage services are common to both (see below).

Of course that is not to say that e-books and e-journals are entirely a new concept. As we noted in Chapter 1, Project Gutenberg distributed its first e-text in the early seventies, the same decade that saw the formation of Oxford University's e-text archive (**http://ota.ahds.ac.uk/**). ARPANET, the first manifestation of the internet, was being used for distribution of pre-prints in the 1960s, and in the 1970s projects such as the EIES (Electronic Information Exchange System) and BLEND (Birmingham Loughborough Electronic Network Development) saw initial explorations of the use of e-journals as a replacement for paper journals. Indeed perhaps the earliest true e-journal was unsurprisingly called *EJournal* (ISSN 1054–1055, starting out as *Credo1.net*) in 1989. This was published and distributed by the University at Albany, SUNY, and was 'concerned with the implications of electronic networks and texts'.

At present both media are causing considerable concern. Jeff Slagell amusingly painted this scenario:

Anyone who works in a serials department will tell you that his domain is the library equivalent of the Wild West. The steady stream of new issues is constantly interrupted by delayed publications, title changes, out-of-control subscription prices, and difficult collection develop- ment decisions. It's in this environment that journals have acquired the reputation of a gang of outlaws for many librarians. They reappear every year and demand more money, while stealing from equally important parts of the materials budget.

The advent of electronic journals has only magnified the problem. These digital bandits brandish different formats and pricing schemes, making their selection and organization increasingly difficult.

(Slagell, 2001, 35)

To this band of desperados, we can add e-books, fellow outlaws or 'digital bandits'.

What is an e-book?

An e-book is an electronic representation of a book, usually a parallel publication of a print copy, but occasionally 'born digital'. Generally, though, e-books refer to products that appear as single titles, and in terms of subject matter these are usually as fiction or textbooks. The new *Concise Oxford English dictionary* (2001) defines an e-book as: 'an electronic version of a printed book which can be read on a personal computer or handheld device designed specifically for this purpose'. According to Ormes (2000): 'the term e-book is used specifically to describe a text which requires the use of e-book software or hardware to read'. She notes, however, that the term can also refer to the hand-held device used to read the texts. However, like her this book will refer to these as 'e-book readers' to avoid confusion.

At present the use of e-books is relatively low (e.g. in the USA in 2000 there was an annual turnover of $12m, as opposed to the $32bn print market), yet it is often predicted that this will change (rising, according to some forecasters, to around $8bn by 2005).

The market for e-books is very new, but at the same time seems to be in constant change. In August 2000 Microsoft released their version of an e-book reader, and in the same month we witnessed one of the many corporate takeovers when Adobe acquired Glassbook. Only a few weeks later Barnes and Noble bought out Fatbrain and Mighty Words, and then in November RCA bought up Rocketboot. To get an idea of the complexity of this one need only take a look at the e-book industry map (**www.ebookmap.net**) with an astonishing list of publishers, suppliers, intermediaries, production agencies, and so on.

How do you use an e-book?

One of the main considerations for the person charged with building a collection of electronic resources is how the user will access any dataset purchased, and with e-books this is more complicated than usual. Most commonly there are five ways that people use e-books:

1   online via the web
2   by downloading to a standard PC (or Mac) and reading them via their operating systems
3   by downloading them and reading them on generic PDAs (personal digital assistants, or handheld computers)
4   by downloading them and reading them on specific devices used for e-books
5   by printing them to paper, i.e. utilizing POD (print on demand).

Before we consider what the implications of these are to the librarian, let us look at them in slightly more detail.

Via the web

At present the reading of e-books via a standard web browser seems to be in keeping with the general moves for online delivery. The web interface allows the user to read the text, of course, but it also opens up possibilities of linking to other resources, cross-text searching, utilization of dictionaries and so on. NetLibrary and Questia are two examples of companies that offer web access to e-books.

Downloading to a PC (or Mac)

This involves the reader downloading the e-book from an internet e-book service (e.g. Amazon), and interacting with it via a dedicated piece of software. Examples of such applications are the 'readers' produced by Microsoft and Adobe (the latter's was formerly known as Glassbook). Market research indicates that this method of accessing e-books is potentially as large as using the web, with estimated figures placing current ownership of PCs in the US alone at 200 million, with 80% of those already using Adobe's Acrobat reader.

Downloading to hand-held readers

Palm Pilots and PDAs provide another means of accessing e-books. Here we can see utilization of a gradually emerging piece of hardware generally used for note-taking and calendars. These hand-held machines allow users to read e-books as long as they have a specific piece of software installed (e.g. Microsoft's Reader). The distinction between these devices and e-book readers, however, is not always so clear cut. The Franklin eBookMan started life as an e-book reader, but has functions that would usually be associated with a generic PDA. Overall this is a promising area (though nowhere near as large as the potential offered by web access).

Downloading to e-book-specific devices

At present on the market there are specific pieces of hardware that are designed solely for reading e-books. The largest company involved in this is Gemstar, which bought up the ground-breaking Rocketbook reader series. At the time of writing [September 2001] Gemstar have two models on the market, both of which use proprietary formats to store and deliver the e-book. The question is why anyone would choose to go down this singular hardware route when the options above allow for much wider use. The answer may lie in the advantages offered by e-book-specific devices:

1 they have larger screens and better interfaces
2 they are light and portable
3 they provide good storage (up to 350 titles at a time) with an extensive battery life (approaching 40 hours before they need recharging)

y provide additional functions not offered by the desktop readers
ed above.

However, it has to be said that many observers remain to be convinced by
these arguments. The long-term future for such devices is very much in
question if one considers that only around 100,000 have been sold in the
US so far (though of course the market is relatively new). However, new
products such as the *hie*book reader (which also allows the user the
additional functionality of playing MP3 files) and the goReader (which is
a larger, tablet-sized device aimed at the textbook market) show promising signs for future developments.

Print on demand

Although the e-book is a digital resource, some readers will still want
print copies. Therefore many services also offer the user the option of
selecting an e-book but having a paper copy sent to them, hence the term
print on demand. Companies that specialize in this include InstBooks,
ODMS, Sprout, and NetLibrary.

Standards

The file format for e-books varies, and the standards that are being
adopted by publishers and how easy it is for these to be used, and
migrated to or from, are of concern. With e-journals, as we shall see, the
majority of publishers seem to be settling on PDF for the time being
(though some will offer Postscript, TeX, or LaTeX alternatives). With e-
books PDF is certainly an option, and is on offer by some publishers
(Adobe for one, of course, with its Electronic Book Exchange or EBX
standard), but other standards are also being developed. A common one
is the OeB ('Open e-book' – **www.openebook.org/**) which is based on
XML (the Extensible Mark-Up Language, the next generation of SGML,
or Standard Generalized Mark-Up Language), an attractive option to
those worried about long-term use. This is the standard being used by
Microsoft for their reader and .lit files.

Implications for collection developers

What implications will the above have for the librarian or collection developer? There are many pluses, of course. As Chapman (2001, 94) notes, e-books should help in the area of pre-prints, and will look extremely attractive to the student market. However, the biggest problem collection developers may face is actually locating the e-book of choice. Sites such as ebookAd (**www.ebookad.com/**) will provide some starting points, but the traditional catalogues, books in print datasets, and other A&I services will not be of much use. National deposit libraries are still only running a voluntary deposit of e-books, so even their extensive catalogues are hardly comprehensive in this field. Furthermore, we will see later on that the way e-books are marketed will also pose specific problems. For the time being, however, we should concentrate on how e-books are delivered (i.e. the five methods noted above) and see what problems these will pose for the collection developer.

By far the simplest method is web delivery, and here we are simply facing problems of licensing and authentication. Next comes the 'downloading to a PC or Mac'. Two problems arise here (outside of authentication and misuse through copying). First, who is given permission to do the downloading? Cost implications mean this will probably be restricted in most cases to a person in authority, rather than allowing anyone to download. Second, as noted in the previous chapter, any use of third-party proprietary software (in this case the 'e-book readers') has hidden costs and requires someone to download and install the application, and to make sure it is maintained.

With hand-held devices (such as PDAs or e-book-specific devices) the problems increase dramatically, particularly when it comes to circulation. Ormes (2000) notes two possible methods:

1   Circulation of e-book readers (or PDAs). Here the actual hardware itself with the e-book of choice on it will be lent to the user. There are considerable problems with this, of course, not only arising from the potential loss or damage to the device itself, but also due to the fact that many downloadable e-books are locked to the specific reader they are first put on. The librarian, therefore, would need to keep an

administrative record of all the e-books they have bought and on what machines they are held.

2   Circulation of e-books – some systems will allow for this, whereby the e-book can be lent out as a file with an encrypted certificate. Advanced systems such as those being offered by NetLibrary will allow the collection manager to run (virtually) a checking in and out service, and to stop access to a book (which is retained online) for specific users. Here the e-book is not actually circulated as such, though, it is more a case that there is a means of controlling access.

Ormes is correct to note that there are also major advantages offered to librarians by e-books:

1   stock selection can be driven purely by demand, and new books can be purchased within minutes:

> The instant access of e-books has strong implications for the traditional collection development model. Public libraries tend to buy most books using the just-in-case model. Books are bought in expectation of demand. The librarians choose what they think their public wants to or even should be reading. Developing an e-book collection could mean moving to a just-in-time model – with the readers' demands being met within minutes of their requests. This would mean that the library more accurately buys books which its users want.   (Ormes, 2000)

2   possible future savings, as the cost of e-books is expected to fall below that of a printed book
3   the absence of a choice between hardback and paperback
4   durability – the e-book will not degrade and therefore does not need conservation (though one should note the discussions on archiving in the previous chapter)
5   space – an e-book takes up relatively little physical space (in theory only that of the medium it is stored on, i.e. the e-book reader or the desktop PC).

What is an e-journal?

Now let us consider a range of similar questions when it comes to e-journals. In the previous chapter it was stated that e-journals are simply electronic representations of a journal. This is undoubtedly a simplification of many of the issues. The library at the University of Glasgow provides its readers with the following definition:

> Any journal that is available over the Internet can be called an 'electronic journal'. In some cases, print equivalents exist; in some cases, not. Some electronic journals (e-journals) are freely available; others have charging mechanisms of different types. Some are issued by established publishers; others are produced from an individual academic's office. As with print journals, the quality and relevance of e-journals can vary considerably.
>
> (University of Glasgow Library,
> **www.lib.gla.ac.uk/Enquiries/faqwhat.html#E-Journal**)

This illustrates some of the many problems that surround e-journals at the moment – their association with print copies, the range in pricing models, the provenance of many titles – and these will be discussed later on in this chapter. At least, however, we are reasonably familiar with the types of product we will be dealing with. Journals (both print and electronic) present us with a collection of articles under a recognized title. This in turn presents the reader with information on the expected quality of the article (linked to the reputation of the publishing house, the peer-reviewing scheme, and so on – see Morris, 2000). As we shall see, e-journals can be purchased in the same way as print journals, i.e. through direct means or via a subscription agent or other intermediary. In other words for someone new to buying e-journals, but familiar with traditional methods of subscribing to serials, much of the following will seem reassuringly familiar. Yet at the same time there are important differences that should be taken into account.

Like e-books, e-journals offer many advantages, the most obvious ones being:

- speed of access to the latest information (particularly relevant in the business and science sectors)
- ability to implement multimedia elements
- quick searching
- linking from and to other resources
- security (i.e. e-journals can't be 'lost')
- single user or location restrictions don't apply
- downloading an article to a personal computer for later use or printing is easier (than photocopying or scanning).

It has been argued that the main advantage of e-journals over their print counterparts is that they are interactive, or at least offer an element of interactivity (see Liew et al., 2000). As with e-books, e-journals seem to be in a continual state of flux – hardly surprising as they have not been with us for too long (in any sizeable amount that is), as illustrated by the following note from 1994:

> Electronic journals are at the centre of moves by three prominent scientific information providers, Elsevier, Chapman & Hall, and ISI. Elsevier will launch its first e-journal early next year, titled *Immunology Today*. Using OCLC's electronic journal system, this will combine elements of the printed journals, such as peer review, with elements unique to the e-journal — past articles, hypertext links, news, product information and a list of the latest vacancies for immunologists around the world.   (*Information World Review*, November 1994)

In other words, the appearance of an e-journal was considered 'news' only seven years ago. We can consider this alongside a more recent press release: 'Sage Publications has reached an agreement with Ingenta, the global research gateway, to provide electronic access to over 230 Sage journals published from their London and California offices' (posted on the **e-collections@ jiscmail.ac.uk** list, 9 March 2001). This repeats the point made in the last chapter about the separation of data (in this case the Sage journals) from the supplier or interface (i.e. Ingenta above). We will look at this in more detail later on.   .

For the purposes of this book, however, we will return to the simplest of definitions. That is to say, when we are discussing an e-journal we are looking at an electronic publication that is produced as a series. For the present we do not need to worry about the association with the printed version (if there is one), and in keeping with this book the discussion will be limited to titles that are marketed, i.e. those that the collection developer may consider purchasing.

How do you use e-journals?

Pedley (2001) outlined a series of scenarios where an e-journal might be encountered:

1   The publisher sends out a PDF file (for use with Adobe's Acrobat reader) containing the complete issue (push technology)
2   The publisher sends out an e-mail stating that a new issue is available on their website (a combination of push and pull technology)
3   The publisher announces by e-mail that a new article or section has been added to the website
4   The website is only a supplement to the hard copy (it contains merely a selection of articles, or ones from previous issues)
5   Articles are made available via an intermediary agent such as Catchword or Ingenta.

Once again several points of interest arise from this brief list. Although PDF is by no means the only way e-journals are published it is becoming the norm, and we have already seen (with e-books above) the effects this might have on the local institution's resources. The second and third points indicate something that is very apparent in e-journals, namely the idea that a journal can now be bought (or viewed) article by article, whereas in the print world the purchaser had to buy and retrieve the entire issue (there is a similarity here with e-books in the sense that the latter, especially with fiction, can be issued a chapter at a time). The fifth point in the list is of interest as it highlights the role of third-party agents (arising from our observation in the previous chapter that in the electronic world the data is often separated from the supplier).

Yet we should not lose sight of the fact that in the vast majority of cases people will access the e-journal via a standard web browser, which may or may not launch the Acrobat reader. At present, in contrast to e-books, there are no such things as e-journal-specific readers, or any utilization of the hand-held device for distributing articles. That is not to say that it will never happen, and there are signs that magazines and newspapers are interested in taking their experiments with WAP technology (the Wireless Application Protocol aimed at the mobile phone market) further by looking to deliver to the individual (via a PDA, for example). When it comes to academic journals, however, mainly because they are licensed to libraries and not to individuals, the predominant delivery platform is the web.

Linkage services

It is appropriate at this point to look more closely at the idea of linkage services, as this follows on naturally from our discussion of accessing and using e-journals. Although it is often entirely feasible to point the user directly to the website of the journal publisher, there are other opportunities offered by abstracting and indexing services. That is to say, users can link directly from bibliographic citations to the full text of the articles. Before we move on to discuss this in more detail let us recap on the three types of linkage service that are available:

1   where websites mutually link to each other to help advertise
2   where a service, such as an abstract and indexing resource, links directly to more content (usually full-text)
3   where cross referencing within a resource (such as an article) is facilitated (as offered by the Catchword service).

For the purposes of this book, the latter two are the main concern. From the outset it should be noted that linking in this sense, which allows direct access to full-text articles or numerical data, is highly desired by the user. It assists readers in navigation (by allowing them to get quick and direct access to the expanded resource), it adds value to the content of both the indexing service and the full-text articles (by allowing at least two points of access), and therefore increases the overall use of both.

Example

A user is searching through an A&I service building up a series of citations that he would like to look at. Many of these are only available in print form, but some have been published electronically also. If the host institution (i.e. the one where the user is based) has a subscription to the electronic journals then a linkage service would allow him to automatically go from the citation to the full text of the article.

Linking can be defined in two ways: direct and indirect. The former takes the user directly to the expanded object within the same environment (i.e. the publisher of an A&I service also publishes the e-journal, allowing direct linking to the full text). Indirect linking involves the use of two or more separate services, for example where the A&I service (owned by one company) integrates with the institution's OPAC, a third-party catalogue, thus allowing the reader direct access to the holdings of the host library. This scenario can become more complicated when there are a multitude of services involved (e.g. the A&I service, the OPAC, third-party publishers or aggregators providing the e-journals with the full text, or print-on-demand services). This structural complexity may be confusing to the user, especially if it involves a series of authentication processes at each stage. Furthermore, it is also difficult to keep track of administratively.

The main problem surrounding these services arises from the fact that linking does not necessarily guarantee access, i.e. at some point the reader may try to follow a link to a service to which the host institution has not subscribed. This, of course, can prove to be extremely frustrating to the user who may not realize why access is being denied. This results from the fact that there are two models for implementing a linkage service (dictated to the librarian by the publisher, alas). The first model is preferred by many collection developers as users are only shown links to full text articles to which the institution has subscribed. In other words, there are links to 'mutual subscriptions', or the links could be said to be 'appropriate'. As long as the system by which this is administered is kept simple, this clearly is a desirable step forward. With the second model, though, links are provided to all the titles *potentially* available under the agreement, regardless of whether the institution has subscribed to them or not. It is with this model ('inappropriate linking') that many problems arise. In its favour, though, the local institution is relieved of any administrative burden, as subscription monitoring is unnecessary.

Apart from inappropriate linking, problems also arise with maintaining links (i.e. the responsibility for this), making sure they are context-sensitive, and somehow integrating it all with the systems based at the local institution. To this end it is worth keeping an eye on the developments of the SFX system, which now comes under the umbrella of ExLibris (**www.sfxit.com/body.html**). This uses the OpenURL standard and is aimed at 'seamlessly linking heterogeneous scholarly information resources, whether these are hosted by the library and/or by external information providers; and regardless of format and communications protocol' (working both with DOIs – digital object identifiers (**www.doi.org/**) – and SIDs, server IDs: two more stable ways of identifying and managing digital content). If this sounds too technical, then do not worry. The main lesson to take from this is that publishers recognize many of the problems that the current technologies present to the librarian, and are seeking to develop new systems (such as SFX) which will make, for example, linking from citations to full text much more easy to implement, much more robust, and above all appropriate.

As we have noted earlier, whatever the problems, the idea behind linking between A&I databases, the full text of the journal articles, OPACs, print-on-demand services, and so on is strongly supported by readers. Therefore the collection developer will often experience considerable pressure to buy in such a service. At present, linkage services have tended to concentrate on the e-journal market but it is clear they offer considerable benefits for e-book use also.

Buying e-books and e-journals

So far we have concentrated on the differences between e-books and e-journals. It is now time to look again at some of the similarities. The most striking correlation lies in the purchasing of these products. To put it succinctly, the marketing of e-books and e-journals will be affected to varying degrees by:

1   whether the data is being marketed to an individual or an institution
2   whether there is an explicit relationship in the licence between print subscriptions and that of the online version
3   whether the material can be bought piecemeal (i.e. article-by-article or chapter-by-chapter) or as a whole.

Although it is feasible to buy directly from publishers in terms of e-books and e-journals (and in some cases that is the only option), more often than not licences will be dealt with by a subscription agent or aggregator. This is clear evidence of one of the 'issues' raised in the previous chapter, namely that of the ease with which the data itself (in this case the articles and textbooks) is separated from the supplier. Publishers are quite willing to market their texts via a variety of third-party agents or intermediaries and regularly do so. On their part, customers who are used to dealing with such parties in the print arena are also often keen to purchase via this route in the electronic world.

Overall it can also be said that this has led to a shift from purchasing by title and subject area to mass deals by aggregators based around a particular publisher's holdings.

Kidd and Prior (2000) note the services that the Association of Subscription Agents (ASA) state that their members should offer. The advantages to the collection developer, then, are that a subscription agent should:

1 maintain up-to-date journal and price information
2 keep information on the availability and prices of electronic journals and provide advice on their licensing and access
3 provide clear, detailed invoices noting customers' special requirements

4 process and order efficiently new subscriptions
5 renew subscriptions in good time
6 respond effectively to claims for missing issues.

(Kidd and Prior, 2000, 83)

Other advantages are an overall simplified means of access, the monitoring of usage statistics, and (possibly) long-term archiving of copies. Both e-books and e-journals are available through these agencies, and many people purchase their collections through them. In the case of e-journals many names are familiar (though new agents have appeared that cover just the electronic market, such as Stanford University's HighWire Press). However, with e-books, because of the relatively fledgling state of the market, new intermediaries are appearing (and disappearing) all the time.

There are, though, some notable differences in the way e-books and e-journals are marketed. A minor one, for example, would be the need to check whether membership of a particular society has an effect on the price of an e-journal subscription. This will probably not be an issue with e-books. Second, we have already noted the possibility of virtually 'unbinding' a journal so that one can buy on an article-by-article basis, and this is also appearing with e-books (especially fiction), where the user can buy on a chapter-by-chapter basis. Yet with the latter this can be taken much further. If we look at the marketing stance of the e-book firm Questia, for example, we can see that it is clearly aimed at the single consumer who wishes to purchase textbooks one at a time. Furthermore, when we consider the systems offered by online bookstores such as Amazon or Barnes and Noble, where users can buy a text and download it straight to their PC or e-book reader, then the gap between this and the purchasing of e-journals widens. In the case of eBrary, which is offering the possibility of micro-transactions (small charges and payments resulting from downloads), we may even witness publishing on a paragraph-by-paragraph basis. It is clear that one model will win through.

However, it is not unrealistic to see a future wherein both e-books and e-journals will be sold both on a library licence basis (i.e. bulk purchasing of titles from the publisher or an intermediary) and to individuals on a piecemeal basis.

Print and electronic

One of the main issues collection developers face when buying e-journals is the association between print and electronic, though this has not been prominent in the e-book arena. In other words, licensing deals are being drawn up by publishers which make an explicit link between subscribing to the print version of a journal and the electronic one. In some cases a subscription to the former may give free access to the e-version, or at the very least a discount for accessing the digital copy. In some cases access to the electronic copy is only available to those that subscribe to the print version; indeed in the most extreme case the publisher refuses to allow cancellation of the print subscription even if the e-journal has been paid for. Either way, though, the publisher is attempting to maintain the sales of print copies. Atherton (2001) noted: 'Of around 10,000 electronic journal titles currently available, 66% are available with a print subscription at no extra cost, but there is a move towards "pay per view", with 53% of publishers already using this form of charging' (reporting a talk by C. Jones, Swets Blackwell).

This link (if it is enforced by the publisher) can present significant problems for the collection developer:

1   Theoretically an advantage of the e-journal is that one can cancel the print copy, saving both money and shelf space; the former at least is lost if both subscriptions have to be maintained.
2   In a dispersed organization where subscriptions are taken out by individual departments, the administrative burden of collating all print purchases, and the negotiations with the publisher to see if this satisfies the licence conditions, can be considerable.
3   Taxation laws for particular countries can lead to further confusion (such as value added tax in the UK, which is not charged on print subscriptions).

Above all, the concept that a print subscription must be retained is entirely against the ethos behind electronic publishing. At best it can be seen as the publisher attempting to prop up the print market. At worst it is a cynical attempt by them to extract even more money from the consumer.

The dog fights back

The way that journal (both print and electronic) marketing has been handled by publishers over the last few years has led many customers, and would-be suppliers of articles, to seriously question the long-term validity of the models on offer. There is a perception that publishers are pursuing a pricing model based entirely on the medium and not on the content. On the whole the deals are seen to be overly complicated, administratively a burden, restrictive, and of course, too expensive. As Meadows (2000) notes: 'The base difficulty with all these price increases is that they have exceeded the growth in purchasing power not only of many individuals, but even of many institutions' (p. 7).

To put this in perspective, according to the Scholarly Publishing and Academic Resources Coalition (SPARC – **www.arl.org/sparc/**) the average price of an academic journal went up by 207% between 1986 and 1999. As Steven Harnard suggested with the following sobering prediction:

> The data will show that even the very richest institutions, with the biggest S/L/P [subscription, licences, pay-per-view] budgets (e.g., Harvard), will only be able to afford a minority of the total relevant annual corpus. And most institutions will be able to afford much less.
>
> This means that MOST of the refereed research literature is inaccessible to MOST researchers on the planet – which is particularly scandalous, given that ALL of that literature is a give-away FROM all those researchers, and that there is no longer any reason, hence any justification, whatsoever, for ALL of them not having access to ALL of it, for free, right now.
>
> (message posted to **lis-elib@jiscmail.ac.uk**, 15 January 2001)

Moreover an extreme view (but one which many people hold) would suggest that the people who write the articles for journals find themselves in the situation of:

• having to agree to restrictive conditions whereby they will have great difficulty in reusing or reprinting their own work

- having to buy back their own work from the publisher (or at least their institution or library will need to)
- receiving very little reward (financially that is) for their work whilst witnessing high profits made by the publishers
- increasingly having to take on more and more of the duties that one would expect of publishing houses of old (i.e. proofreading, making corrections, producing camera-ready copy).

This is particularly pertinent if the article is being written by a researcher for an academic journal with limited circulation. The writer will probably receive no money at all for his or her work, and will see it appear in a medium that is being purchased less and less. In fact the only reasons academics might choose to pursue this route are: (a) they consider it the only avenue open to them (and traditionally this has been true) to have their work read as widely as possible, and (b) there is pressure on them to publish their research from various internal and external assessment agencies.

To some, then, the publisher of academic journals is the parasitic flea living on the back of the dog. It lives off the work of researchers but provides them with very little reward for their endeavours, and seeks to lock them into various agreements that prohibit reuse of their work. Yet the world of e-journals is perhaps at last offering the dog an opportunity to bite back.

The following extract (dating from 1998) is indicative of the way many people were and are thinking:

Two physics societies are combining to launch a free electronic journal which they claim will offer an alternative to high-priced hard copy counterparts. Behind the New Journal of Physics, to be launched this autumn, are the Institute of Physics [**www.iop.org/**] and Deutsche Physikalische Gesellschaft, the German Physical Society. According to the two societies, most university libraries' budgets have not kept pace with the rising cost of scientific journals, with the result that many are forced to cancel their subscriptions to one or more physics journals each year. By launching the electronic-only journal of research articles on the internet they hope to 'put a stop to the price spiral'. Free to users, the publication will be financed by article charges paid by the authors.   (*Information World Review*, May 1998)

This stance has attracted much support, as witnessed by the discussions on the American Scientist Forum 'For whom the gate tolls?' (starting in September 1998 – see **http://amsci-forum.amsci.org/archives/ september98-forum.html**). In other words, because anyone can publish online via the internet, the onus is shifting to the publishers to justify exactly what services they are offering. Meadows (2000) is right to observe that: 'Ultimately, the success or otherwise of electronic journals depends on the attitude of authors. No input of material: no journals' (p.11).

Perhaps this could be modified by saying that the future of 'commercially published electronic journals' is under question. The recent formation of the Public Library of Science in 2001 (**www. publiclibraryofscience.org/**) is a further example of this emerging feeling. Primarily concerned with free access to past research and its archiving (whilst recognizing that publishers have a right to 'a fair financial return for their role in scientific communication') they state that:

> we will publish in, edit or review for, and personally subscribe to, only those scholarly and scientific journals that have agreed to grant unrestricted free distribution rights to any and all original research reports that they have published, through PubMed Central and similar online public resources, within 6 months of their initial publication date.   (**www.publiclibraryofscience.org/plosLetter.htm**)

By 2001 this open letter had been signed by 24,931 people from 166 countries. To this we can add the Scholarly Publishing and Academic Resources Coalition and the eprints.org (**www.eprints.org/**) venture to allow self-archiving by the author or institution in order to free up refereed research material (see also the Open Archives initiative – **www. openarchives.org/**). In a similar light we could also consider the recent outrage expressed by customers at the price *Nature* was attempting to market its e-product. As was reported in the *Times Higher Education Supplement*: 'Nature Online which attempted to market at 30 pence per person on campus ran into great resistance. Partly because of cost, but also because the contents of the on-line version had a 3-month delay on news' (C. Davis, 'College libraries snub pricey online journal', 2 March 2001, p. 4).

The situation was made worse by the fact that *Science* (the US equivalent of *Nature*) did not have a three-month delay, and was approximately half the price. The subsequent (and successful) veto of the licence until the price was reduced is a further example of the growing empowerment of the user community due to the move to digital publishing. For a comprehensive discussion of this area (plus a discussion of pre-print and post-print) see Steve Harnard's papers on electronic publishing (**http://cogsci.soton. ac.uk/~harnad/**). Professor Harnard also provides links to two other 'exemplars' at the University of Southampton in this area – *Cogprints* (Cognitive Science Eprint Archive, **http://cogprints.soton.ac.uk/**) and *Psycoloquy* (a refereed online journal in the area of psychology, cognitive science, etc., **www.cogsci.soton.ac.uk/psycoloquy/**).

Chapter summary

In this chapter we have concluded our discussion of the landscape of electronic resources (begun in the previous chapter) with an extended analysis of e-books and e-journals. We have covered the following:

1   the similarities and differences between e-journals and e-books
2   purchasing and using both products
3   the implications both have for collection developers
4   some possible future trends in e-publishing of journals.

Having gained a general perspective of the issues and products, it is now time to look at the complete life cycle of building up a collection of electronic resources.

4 What to buy? Assessing and acquiring the dataset

Introduction

So far we have been concentrating on introducing the beginner to the various electronic resources available for purchase. It is the contention of this author that this is absolutely crucial. Without an awareness of the range of products, their particular nuances, and the overall problems that emerge when moving to acquiring digital material, the collection developer cannot be expected to make informed decisions when evaluating and purchasing these resources. It is now time, however, to turn more fully to the task of building up the digital collection itself.

The life cycle of digital collection development

In Chapter 1 we argued that building up a library of digital resources had many similarities to traditional collection development, though at the same time there were some notable differences. At that point we suggested the stages involved in collection development (p. 6). It is now time to look at these in more detail with reference to digital resources. In Figure 4.1 the steps involved in acquiring a digital resource are outlined in full, up to the point where the invoice is paid (note that there are significant steps to be taken after this point which will be discussed in Chapter 5).

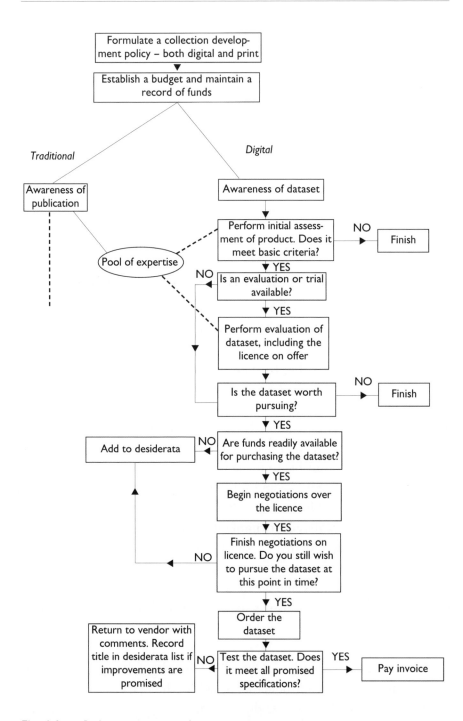

Fig. 4.1   *Preliminary stages in dataset acquisition*

General comments

To begin with it is clear that there are two 'paths' or tracks apparent in Figure 4.1. The first represents traditional content development (i.e. print resources) and the second, more developed one, concentrates on the digital arena. Both can be seen to stem from the same collection development policy, and, as is increasingly the norm, from the same budget. Furthermore, central to both is a pool of expertise consisting of subject specialists, users, technical experts, and so on. These 'stakeholders', that is to say the people involved in the decision-making process, will be discussed in Chapter 5.

Formulating a collection development policy

It cannot be stressed enough that the collection development policy for digital materials must be part of the overall strategy in terms of acquisitions for your company or department (e.g. see the Arizona State Library's guides, **www.dlapr.lib.az.us/cdt/slrer.htm**, where this link is reinforced). This is the first step in Figure 4.1 from which the two paths branch. This is increasingly important now that the link between print and electronic (as with e-journals) has become more and more established. Furthermore any policy arrived upon should be made as public as possible (or at least available to the appropriate communities that will be affected by it). For a concise and simple example of such a public statement see Emory University's 'Collection development policy' (**http://academic.uofs.edu/organization/codes/emory.html**).

The collection development policy needs to cover many things, but at its root there should be a clear account of where the institution currently is in terms of its holdings, and where it wishes to be. The following quote is illustrative of the types of issues you may wish to include in an opening declaration:

> Over the next two years, Cornell University Library (CUL) will position itself for the introductory decade of the 21st century. In an age characterized by burgeoning digital technology, CUL will provide its faculty, students, and staff with expanded access to an increasingly rich

array of electronic information resources. The result will be a superior library service offering a knowledge base suited to supporting the mission of a world-class university. To achieve this goal, the library has designed an ambitious strategic plan.   (Cornell University Library)

How do you now begin to form a more comprehensive collection plan? If the institution is starting from scratch and like most places in part (at least) is disparate in its infrastructure (i.e. there are subdepartments or libraries with their own budgets), then it is highly probable that there will be existing subscriptions in place already. The first step in formulating the policy, then, is to collate all this information to produce a clear picture of what is already subscribed to, and why (a simple cost–benefit analysis). This survey should also try to discover where the existing digital collections, if any, are strong, where they show a weakness or gap, how they complement the print collections, who is paying for what and for how long they are committed, and so on. With e-journals (and e-books) there may also be links to print subscriptions to take into account. Ideally, if the nature of the institution allows, this information should be brought together in a single location, and a central repository of all existing licences and other documentation should be created.

Once an overall picture of the current state of play has been established you can now consider more strategic level decisions. In particular, how far down the road of digital collection development do you want to travel? This is perhaps the fundamental problem, and there are many questions and issues which arise from this one simple query, some of which are listed below. If there is no clear picture of where the digital resource collection is heading, and how it will interface with more traditional collections, experience has shown that resources will start to appear in an idiosyncratic fashion, without any cohesive policy in terms of targeting areas or matching priorities. Let us list some of the main questions which you may wish to answer in a collection development statement. In terms of building electronic resources you could ask:

1   Where do you want to be in one year, two years, five years, and how do you wish to get there?

2   Are you aiming to rid yourself of as much print material as possible and replace it with electronic versions?

3   How will the funding for this be made available – via reallocation, raising new funds, or cutting subscriptions elsewhere?

4   What is the nature of your reader community?

5   Are they all based locally or will some require remote access?

6   Will they be happy with pay-per-use systems, and, more importantly, will you?

7   How good is your IT infrastructure and support?

8   Can they be relied upon to deliver the material successfully and adequately?

When you are looking at gaps and weaknesses in the collection it is easiest to work on a subject category basis. Yet some observers have noted that this can pose difficulties and favour an approach centred on the type of material (e-books, e-journals, etc.) rather than traditional discipline divides.

In recent discussions (e.g. Weintraub, 1998; Faulkner and Hahn, 2001) collection development policies have been termed 'genre statements'. Simply put, this is a more generic statement that would be of use and interest to readers, people charged with collection development, and publishers. It would encompass such things as the collection development policy statement, licensing details, and so on. In a sense this is a series of documents that seeks to explain to readers and users the general issues surrounding digital collection development, and at the same time justify why certain approaches have had to be adopted. It will also contain all the information needed by suppliers to construct the licence. For an example of a genre statement in action see the one posted by the University of Maryland (**www.lib.umd.edu/UMCP/CLMD/COLL.Policies/epubguide.html**).

Establishing a budget

Let us now turn our attention to the budget. Again, as Figure 4.1 indicates, it is best to see budgetary decisions as relating to overall collection development, and wherever possible to charge a single body with this work. Although it is common practice to then divide the budget it is often not clear as to which way is the best. Should the division be simply between print and electronic (i.e. via material), or should it be by subject? Whichever is chosen it is important that, wherever possible, all expenditure still ultimately comes out of the same overall acquisitions spending, and thus a cohesion between any decision making is enforced. The most obvious reason for this is that a purchase in one area may directly (and immediately) have an impact on policies in the other. For example, a subscription to an electronic resource may immediately make the print version redundant. Alternatively, a decision to cancel a print subscription in the hope of having a purely digital one may be forbidden by the licence agreement (with e-journals some agreements require that the print subscription is maintained). The one thing that can be said to be true with absolute certainty is that 'no acquisitions department would ever describe its budget as being large enough' (Chapman, 2001, 115).

It is usually the case that budgets are decided on an annual basis (either the financial year, calendar year, or academic year), and funds are drawn from this throughout the twelve months as subsequent acquisitions are made. Therefore the onus is on the collection developer to pay invoices, and record the changes to the budget throughout this cycle.

A common question is exactly how much should be set aside for digital collection development per annum. First, money should not be set aside as such but should form part of overall acquisitions. Second, there is no answer to this question! In a sense, we are shooting in the dark, as we do not have many precedents to work with (unlike traditional acquisitions budgets). The observation that 'the conventional approach to budgeting is to take last year's budget' (Clayton and Gorman, 2001, 141) and add, seems almost luxurious in electronic collection development as it is such a new area.

Different institutions will have different priorities, different budgets to command, and will be working under different conditions. A commercial company, for example, may only need a few titles but would expect to have to pay considerably more for these compared with a university, which will usually receive an academic discount. A group of institutions that are in the favourable position of being able to band together to deal on a collective basis may find that they will need less funds than a single institution negotiating individually – and so on.

Yet not providing any answer to this question is hardly helpful. When you are establishing a budget, or putting in for an annual renewal, the following concerns should be taken into account:

1   *Maintaining the status quo.* If you already have a set of electronic products available, the main part of the budget request must be to maintain these subscriptions, or to match these recurrent costs. There is nothing more problematic than cancelling a subscription to a product which readers are using – as it will cause untold trouble for the collection developer. In the main, users are not interested in costs as such, they are simply concerned with getting access to information. If you cut off this source (and this will be made even worse if they know that a competitor or similar institution has access to it) then be prepared for considerable criticism. However, in some circumstances it may be feasible to reduce your recurrent costs by cancelling subscriptions (see Chapter 5).

2   *Essential purchases.* It is clear that at times some titles will appear that are 'must have' purchases. This should be costed into the annual budget. For example, a business dataset may be deemed crucial if a company is to maintain its competitiveness. In the first year of raising funds, essential purchases may form the bulk of the budget request.

3   *Targeting desiderata.* As we will advocate later, it is important to maintain throughout the year a desiderata list of titles that you would like to purchase for which funds are not available at present (or you may not feel that a commitment to purchase can be made until the accounts are stabilized). However, a desiderata list that is never targeted will become stagnant and the people or bodies who proposed the datasets that go to make up such a list will become disillusioned with the process. It is therefore suggested that a reasonable target would be to try to purchase around 25% of the titles on the desiderata list each year.

4   *Price increases.* Undoubtedly budgets will have to take into account price rises (arising from inflation, exchange rate fluctuations, or

publishers simply increasing their charges). It is not enough merely to link this to the basic rate of inflation, as price rises for electronic products are influenced by many international factors. For example, although the United Kingdom has a relatively low inflation rate (below 3% for some time) price increases for electronic products have ranged from 7% to 15% per annum. In some instances prices have doubled in the space of a single year. Although it is impossible to predict such rises, some form of contingency money must be included in the budget request (Chapman, 2001, 115, recommends a figure of 10%).

5 *Unforeseen purchases.* To add to this there is the problem of the sudden appearance of products during the financial year which immediately fall into the category of 'must have' purchases. It is recommended, therefore, that some additional funds should be requested each year to cover for this eventuality.

6 *Special considerations – e-journals.* E-journals will present some specific problems when it comes to assembling a budget. This tends to arise from three main factors:

   i *Their link to print subscriptions,* which can cause particular difficulties. First, it reinforces the need to keep digital collection development in line with traditional collection development (or at least the subscriptions side of things). Second, it is very possible that the institution may be disparate in its organization, and individual departments may maintain subscriptions to particular journals. If this is the case and the electronic subscription is only available to people who also subscribe to the print version, then this will need to be overcome. A solution may be to award money from the acquisitions budget to the individual department on the understanding that it maintains the print subscription. Altern-atively, you could attempt to centralize all subscriptions (be they print or electronic).

   ii *The fact that many e-journals are at present free but may in the future have to be paid for;* this is a noticeable problem that has arisen over the past couple of years. There are no hard-and-fast rules as to when this will happen with a particular set of titles, but collection developers need to be aware that it does occur. It is a further manifestation of the problems associated with meeting user expectation. If readers are using a free e-journal and access to it is then denied because a charge has been imposed by the publisher, they will want to know when the service will be reinstated.

iii *The large amounts of money some publishers charge for the bulk deals.*

In summary, using the points noted above, a quick formula for estimating the annual budget needed for building electronic resources might be:

existing recurrent costs★
+ 'inflation'★ (e.g. 8% of existing recurrent costs)
+ essential purchases
+ 25% of total cost of desiderata list
+ contingency funds (to cover unforeseen purchases, including free e-journals becoming paid-for services)

(★ = not applicable if no subscriptions to electronic services exist at present).

For a much lengthier discussion of budget management, readers are directed to Chapter 8 of *Managing information resources in libraries* (Clayton and Gorman, 2001).

Centralized versus devolved budgets

So far the discussion has skirted round the issue of who actually holds the budget. The above comments imply that a single body can make decisions about budgetary matters, purchases, and so on. In other words, the above model is geared towards working with a single centralized budget. However, it is clear that many institutions are disparate in their organization, with departments holding their own budgets, i.e. there is a devolved system. Although this gives departments considerable autonomy in controlling their own financial matters, and protects smaller departments from having their budgets swallowed up by larger, more powerful sections, it does present considerable problems when it comes to purchasing electronic products, many of which (by their very nature) straddle disciplines and departments. As the PURCEL (2000) project observed: 'There is an identifiable tension between the typical funding models . . . driven by institutional culture and structures focused around separate subject disciplines, and the volatile, multi-disciplinary, commercially driven electronic information products' (p. 36).

Although devolved budgets were (and still are in some quarters) very popular it is a fair generalization to say that they do not sit well with building digital resources. As the PURCEL report noted 'there is recognition among HEIs that they are being pushed towards re-centralisation of database and serials funding' (p. 36). There is no easy solution to this as such, as local factors may prohibit any form of centralization. If this is the case then it is recommended that a system is developed wherein all the stakeholders and controllers of budgets can easily keep each other informed of their intentions.

Awareness of the dataset

Assuming that an overall plan for collection development has been established and a budget has been finalized, you are now ready to target new titles for purchasing. There appear to be three main sources of information relating to new datasets:

1   publicity flyers from publishers
2   word of mouth, i.e. e-mail lists, meetings, and websites (such as *NewJour* for new serials on the internet – **http://gort.ucsd.edu/ newjour/NewJourWel.html**)
3   notification by readers and colleagues.

The first two activities constitute one's own research and are proactive. The third scenario (which is reactive) is extremely common, however, and at times can be the most problematic. Here readers, fellow librarians, or company employees may notify the collection developer of a new title and suggest that it is purchased. There may be a limit to the categories of personnel who may offer such suggestions (e.g. a university may not be prepared to receive a proposal from an undergraduate), but that can, at times, be counterproductive. Why, though, might this lead to problems? Surely all information received is welcomed? There are three areas of contention. First, some users may expect that once they propose a dataset it will automatically be purchased. Second, they will wish to be kept informed as to the progress of the dataset, which will require a dissemination exercise. Third, and most commonly perhaps, they will often supply very little information relating to the dataset to accompany the proposal. The first two problems can be overcome by a mixture of user education as to the constraints you are working under, and good communication channels. The last issue again is a problem of user education, but it may be advisable to establish mandatory information which must be part of any proposal before it is considered further. If not, you may have to spend a considerable amount of time chasing up contact details of publishers, pricing structures, and so on. It is suggested that any proposal system (a web-based form may suffice) must require the user to submit the following information:

- name and contact details of proposer
- title of dataset
- brief description of dataset
- publisher and contact details
- price of dataset (including information on networked prices)
- reasons why the dataset has been proposed, and the potential user base.

Assessment, trials and evaluation

Following 'awareness of a dataset', there is the process of actually purchasing the title. Figure 4.1 indicates that the next step is to perform an initial assessment of the product to see if it meets basic criteria. In essence these are the factors that will allow a title onto the desiderata list and those that will exclude it. This generally comes down to three things:

1   cost
2   content
3   capability.

In other words, is the cost of the product within the capacity of the budget? Is its content applicable to the collection development policy? Is there the capability to deliver the product satisfactorily to the end-user (i.e. the 'technical capability' in terms of networks, servers, client machines, authentication systems, and so on)? If the answer to *any* of these is 'no', and moreover one could not envisage a future scenario where this would change, then it may well be the best policy to abandon the pursuit of the title and inform the original proposer. It is worthwhile recording the decision (and the reasons why it was made) for future reference. However, if it looks as though present problems may be overcome in the future (for example a budget increase may make the title affordable) then the product should be added to the desiderata list.

Eventually you will have a list of resources from which (perhaps) a selection needs to be made. These titles will then be looked at more closely with a view to purchasing. This means that a system needs to be in place which enables prioritization between products. The following check-list indicates some of the questions that could facilitate this:

1   Has the dataset been requested by a large number of readers?
2   Will it be heavily used by a large body of readers from all sectors within the institution?
3   Will it provide access to information which is not readily available in other formats?
4   Will it provide a set of tools or features that facilitate and enhance the use of the material?
5   Will it offer the possibility of a potential cost or space saving (e.g. through the cancellation of a print subscription)?
6   Does it have, or is it likely to have, any competitors?
7   Is it essential to maintaining the research profile or competitiveness of a department/faculty/company?
8   Is it based in a subject area that has been relatively underrepresented

by previous dataset purchases?

9 Does it complement an existing digital service?

10 Has it received promises of funding?

11 Is it a one-off purchase (i.e. it does not add to recurrent costs)?

12 Is a consortium deal possible, or is it regarded as good value for money?

None of the above are essential, and different weighting will be attached to the various categories by different types of institutions. Nevertheless, they do illustrate the differing factors that might be considered when prioritizing one title over another.

The next step, once a title has been selected, is to request a trial subscription or evaluation copy. This may not always be possible, in which case the only option is to go by the reputation of the publisher and see if any other institutions have already purchased the product and are using it successfully.

When it comes to the evaluation or trial it is clear that many of the issues discussed later under negotiating the licence will have to be considered. For now, though, we will concentrate on the actual material itself and the system presented to the end-user, and leave aside the licence details. Evaluations and trials are notoriously difficult to organize in terms of actually receiving constructive feedback. The evaluation should draw on a pool of experts and these would ideally represent:

1 subject specialists
2 technical experts
3 readers or reader services
4 interface experts
5 administrative personnel (to consider such things as the implications on the budget, the proposed licence, etc.).

The ideal solution would be to have a core group of expertise covering the last four categories with the ability to bring in subject specialists as applicable, but this may not be practical in smaller institutions. Whatever the make-up of the evaluation group, it must be representative of all the sectors the proposed dataset would have an effect on, i.e. those who will use it, those who will be asked to support it, those who will be asked to network it (or maintain a remote subscription), those who will have to administer the authentication system required, and those who will be asked to pay the money. Moreover, it should be made clear as to who is making this decision, for example: 'Requests for new electronic format products will be reviewed by a committee composed of the Director of Collection Management, the Director of Public Services, and the Head of Systems. If equipment would need to be purchased the request will be reviewed by Directors Council also' (Emory University General Libraries).

The following list of questions provides a fairly comprehensive guide to the types of issues an evaluation might cover. This would also be of use once a dataset has been purchased, at the renewal stage of the life cycle (see Chapter 5). The questions are a collation of work by other institutions drawing on Oxford University's 'Evaluating a dataset' (**www.bodley.ox.ac.uk/dc/eval.htm**), and Harvard's 'Stewards' checklist of questions' (**http://hul.harvard.edu/cmtes/ulc/coers/ checklist.htm**). They reinforce Clayton and Gorman's reflections on the similarities and the differences between selection policies for traditional material and those for electronic products:

> most writers discussing . . . the larger area of electronic resources generally accept that many of the same criteria used to select traditional materials are appropriate for electronic resources. However, 'selecting electronic information resources is inherently more complex than traditional print resources since they involve analysing many other issues such as equipment, space, trade-offs with other resources, technical support, and vendor support.
>
> (Johnson, 1997, quoted in Clayton and Gorman, 2001, 94)

Evaluation checklist

Initial details

- full title of the dataset
- publisher
- details of corresponding print publication (if applicable)
- pricing details:
  — payment model (see section on price beginning on p. 84)
  — standalone cost
  — network cost
  — recurrent or one-off payment
  — additional fees to third parties, or under national taxes
  — (if available) average inflation for product over past few years
- type of product (e.g. CD-ROM plus platform, internet access, tape, etc.)
- machine specifications used for evaluation (include details such as internet connection if applicable)
- date and time of evaluation(s)
- brief description of content.

Setting up or accessing the dataset

Local products

- Is the dataset easy to install?
- Is it easy to network?
- Was all the software needed supplied with the installation CD-ROM?
- Were the instructions clear?
- Does it appear to conflict with other functions of the computer/server?
- Can the dataset be uninstalled easily?

Remote access

- Did you manage to access the site easily?
- Was the URL intuitive?
- Can you bookmark the site or sections of it?
- Does the service use any of the following: frames, cookies, Java, or JavaScript?
- What browsers will it run under, and what version is needed (e.g. Netscape 4.x or higher)?

Both local and remote

- Does the dataset require any plug-ins?
- Does it create an otherwise excessive burden on the client (e.g. requires local disk space)?
- Accessing the opening screen: on average, is this instantaneous, or does it take
  — 1–5 seconds?
  — 5–10 seconds?
  — longer than 10 seconds?
- Accessing the search screen: on average, is this instantaneous, or does it take
  — 1–5 seconds?
  — 5–10 seconds?
  — longer than 10 seconds?
- Have you ever experienced a message saying 'Too many connections/users' ?
- If 'Yes', approximately how often does this occur?
  — rarely (i.e. one access in every ten)?
  — often (i.e. between two and four accesses in every ten)?
  — very often (i.e. 5 or more attempts to access in every ten)?

Coverage

- Is there a clear and easily accessible list of the complete contents of the dataset? If this is a growing resource, or one with updates, how accurate is this list?

- Are there errors noticeable in the text, broken links, or anything else which would indicate a lapse in quality control?
- Would you say that the dataset contains everything that is in the print version (if applicable)? What is the relationship between the electronic product and the print holdings of the institution?
- Have you seen any other publications to compare to this in content? What are they, and how do they compare?
- How often is the product updated?

Interface and searching

- Is there a main menu or some kind of main list that outlines all the functions clearly?
- Is the interface generally easy to use?
- Is navigation intuitive (i.e. does it employ such facilities as 'breadcrumb trails' (navigational aids that inform the user where they are in the hierarchy of the product))?
- Does it conform to accepted standards for disabled access?
- Was it obvious how to browse or start a search?
- Can you:
  — save searches?
  — combine search words?
  — modify searches?
  — narrow/widen searches?
  — use proximity searching?
  — use Boolean operators?
  — truncate search terms and/or use wildcards?
  — limit by year/publication type/language/other?
  — check the indices and pick entries to search for?
  — use any command line searches? Is it made clear how to structure these, or how to use special codes (e.g. au= for author)?
- Can you search the dataset via third-party software (e.g. reference manager tools)?
- Do you get a hint if your search achieved no results?

- Can you see a history of searches?
- Can you save the search set for future use?
- Can users set up or configure personalized accounts?
- Can the dataset be cross-searched with others?
- Sending a simple search and receiving the results (e.g. looking for a term in a single dataset): on average, is this instantaneous, or does it take
  — 1–5 seconds?
  — 5–10 seconds?
  — longer than 10 seconds?

Display/save/print

- Do results display automatically?
- If not, is it intuitive how to access them?
- Is there a choice of formats for display?
- Can you 'mark' useful results?
- How many records can you mark/save/export at once?
- Are the steps for saving/exporting/printing easy to understand?
- Can you save to a floppy disk/hard disk/either?
- Can you e-mail results?
- In what format are records saved (ASCII, .rtf, HTML, other)?
- Can the results be exported to third-party software (e.g. reference manager tools)?

Exiting

- Is it easy to exit/logoff?
- Are you prompted to save or lose your searches/results?
- Is there a timeout system for idle sessions?

Administration

- Is it possible for the administrator to change some settings of the database to suit the users' needs?

- What authentication system is employed (i.e. username/password, simultaneous access, domain name, etc.)?
- Is there a choice of authentication systems on offer?
- Can you add information to the dataset, such as local holdings? Is it easy to interface the dataset with other electronic products?

Documentation and support

- Is any documentation provided?
- Is it sufficient, covering both installation and use?
- Are there customer support and technical support facilities?
- Are these available by telephone/fax/e-mail/the web?
- If there is a website does it include information about system status? (e.g. is the system fully operational? Are connections being refused?, etc.)
- Is there any training available? Is this free of charge?
- If there is an online help system how useful is it?
- How easy is it to access the online help mid-session?
- How closely does it mirror the paper documentation?

General points

- Is this product available on a different platform or through a different aggregator? If so, has this been evaluated?
- Is this publication useful? In other words, could you predict a high demand for it (using existing requests for the product, use/importance of the print publication if applicable, ILL requests, and so on)?
- Would you say this dataset represented good value for money?
- Do you think it will be of use to people in the institution other than the proposer?
- Did you detect any errors or problems either with the actual data or with the search software?
- On average would you envisage using the dataset:
  — less than once a week?
  — 1–3 times per week?

— once a day?

— more than once a day?

This is clearly an extensive list of questions. In most cases it will be extremely difficult to get any feedback from users at all, and such a lengthy questionnaire would stand very little chance of being completed by the average reader. The above then is best seen as the complete picture, but not all of it need be answered by everyone. A technical team or representative may be set certain tasks, as might a subject specialist, or user-interface expert. For the majority, at best only a simple one- or two-sentence response about the product can be expected. The recommendation of this book is to try to form a core evaluation group with responsibility for covering particular sections of the above, with the option of co-opting in subject specialists as appropriate. If the trial is institution-wide a much shorter questionnaire of only three or four questions should be offered in order to receive feedback from the users (they could of course be given the option also to fill in a lengthier evaluation form).

The licence

Part of the evaluation process must include at least a brief glance at the licence the product is being marketed under. At the simplest level the cost of the product must have been considered before proceeding, a detail that will of course be covered in the licence. There is clearly no point in wasting time and effort evaluating a product if you can never possibly afford it (one of our basic criteria noted earlier). Yet eventually a careful consideration of the full licence will have to be undertaken, and this is what we will consider now.

The first thing to remember is that in most cases licences are not set in stone. Individual institutions are always at liberty to discuss and negotiate deals according to their own requirements. Having said that, it is also clear that publishers may respond better to consortia-type bids. If a group of companies or institutions approach a publisher or aggregator with an offer they will stand a good chance of securing the deal they are after under the conditions they want, as they represent the possibility of a large, one-off sale. Ideally this would be done on a national basis. Where this is not possible, though, consortia bids could be put together on a regional or federal basis. If groups are formed, however, it is crucial that during the negotiation stage solidarity is maintained and no-one enters into bilateral agreements. Moreover, any attempt by a publisher to preclude institutions from working together within consortia should be strongly resisted.

It is impossible to predict all the circumstances under which you may be asked to negotiate a deal. Therefore it is perhaps more fruitful to consider the generic issues that may be encountered and need to be addressed in the actual licence itself, i.e. the contract you are asked to sign when purchasing the dataset which details the responsibilities and obligations of both sides (the consumer and the seller).

We are greatly aided in this by the gradual appearance over the years of model licences, which we will discuss shortly. Yet it is worth noting why many have felt the need for such things. In a joint declaration of a model licence by a series of Dutch and German institutions it was noted that: 'university libraries are noticing significant trends as publishers try to erect barriers to the storage and access of information, and present license agreements for the electronic access to journal titles in which additional fees are requested, document delivery is hindered, and non-cancellation clauses are introduced' (Tilburg University, 1997).

Similar sentiments are expressed by Yale University's guidelines:

> As the number of collections in digital formats increase exponentially, more and more libraries and information providers are facing a number of unique challenges presented by this relatively new medium. Chief among these new challenges is crafting agreements with information owners that adequately assure libraries will continue to provide users with comprehensive and timely access to information in digital formats. Because of several unique properties of digital information, agreements that govern the acquisition and maintenance of traditional paper collections are inadequate in the digital information context. Unlike paper materials, digital information generally is not purchased by the library; rather it is *licensed* by the library from information

providers. A license usually takes the form of a written contract or agreement between the library and the owner of the rights to distribute digital information.

(**www.library.yale.edu/~llicense/intro.shtml**)

[consulted September 2001]

This will probably all sound extremely worrying to the newcomer. What should he or she be wary of? What, in turn, do we have a right to expect from a licence?

To begin with, the licence should guarantee a satisfactory quality of service for the subscriber, and it should be clear as to what is allowed and what is not allowed by *both* parties. At the same time the licence has to guarantee the rights and interests of the publisher. All terms and conditions should be clearly spelt out, as should any hidden charges, retroactive costs, and so on. When negotiating a licence you should also be clear as to what are absolutely essential conditions, and what would be good to have but could be forgone.

As noted before, several bodies and institutions have established model licences which can help us in our deliberations. Examples include:

1   'Library licensing principles' (Tilburg University, 1997)
2   Yale University Library's 'Standard license agreement' (**www.library. yale.edu/~llicense/standlicagree.html**); see also the 'CLIR/DLF model license' (**www.library.yale.edu/~llicense/modlic.shtml**)
3   The University of California Libraries' *Principles for acquiring and licensing information in digital formats* (University of California Libraries, 1996)
4   The PA/JISC model site licence (National Electronic Site Licence Initiative).

The following discussion then is a collation of many points covered by these documents (plus some others). It should act as a set of guidelines to the types of issues that will arise, but must also be considered alongside the points raised earlier with the more technical, user-based evaluation of the dataset.

Duration

The licence should clearly state how long the subscriber is tied to the deal and what options are open should there be the wish to cancel the subscription. Simply put, you should be wary of commitment to any deal for a lengthy period of time (over three years, for example). Moreover, there should be clear let-out clauses (and detailed information on refunds) should you feel that the supplier is not honouring their side of the agreement. Similarly, a model licence would contain an agreement by the supplier to renew the licence in the future at an acceptable cost (though it has to be said this is often very hard to secure).

Price

Perhaps the most crucial part of the licence, but at the same time the most difficult to pin down, is the pricing structure. A common question is what is a fair price for an electronic product? The answer to this will always depend on how badly you need the resource, and how much you are willing to pay. The need for a particular resource will depend upon the nature of your institution. A commercial firm, perhaps in the legal or business environment, will have a clear need for a regular newsfeed service, more so than perhaps a creative arts college would do. Similarly, a large A&I service may be crucial to a university in order to maintain its research practices, but not so important to a public library dealing predominantly with non-academics. In other words, in terms of pounds and dollars there is no clear-cut answer. Unfortunately, for the most part, publishers tend not to tailor their pricing structure according to the nature of the institution (outside of the straightforward split between commercial and educational/non-profit deals). The argument that the subject matter in the resource is only of marginal interest, and therefore one should pay only a fraction of the cost compared with an institution where the material might be crucial, will rarely cut much ice.

Pricing is further confused by the fact that there are several models available. These are a crucial part of the licence. In essence the choice is between a one-off fee ('ownership' or 'buying'), which means that the product is purchased outright for use locally, and a recurrent fee (a 'lease license'), i.e. a subscription according to which regular sums of money are paid over an agreed period to maintain access. The latter may also cover updates to the product. It has been known for these two models to be combined. For example, a one-off fee pays for the actual data to be used locally, or to archive, whilst a small subscription is needed to maintain access to a website, or to receive updates. Alternatively, at the end of the lease there may be the option to buy the data completely.

So far so good. However, once we move away from this simple division and consider the various systems that publishers or vendors employ to actually come up with the price (be it one-off or recurrent), then the situation becomes much more complicated. Let us consider some of the ways in which these prices are calculated and presented to the customer, and the potential advantages and disadvantages of each.

A single payment is defined

This is far and away the simplest concept. In short there is a set price for the purchasing of the product, or for an annual subscription to it regardless of predicted use, size of the customer's institution, and so on. How this is controlled will depend upon the authentication system involved either locally or remotely. If you are buying the product for local use, however, be prepared for two prices: one for the standalone version and one for the networked version.

When it comes to e-journals where the licence may be tied to the print subscription, the amount requested can be calculated by a variety of means. It may simply be a percentage of the cost of the print subscriptions already in place. More attractive would be a percentage of the number of titles subscribed to (hence duplicate subscriptions which often occur in large institutions will not increase the price). Or finally it could just be a standard fee which allows access to both print and electronic versions, regardless of the number of print subscriptions or titles held by the institution. This last method, at the time of writing, is the most common deal on offer by publishers.

Advantages

- Single payment is simple and easy to implement.
- It often allows for unlimited use.

Disadvantages

- The system is often inflexible. There is usually very little room for manoeuvre, with smaller institutions finding that they are paying the same amount as larger ones.

Payment depends upon the size of the institution

Here a variable is introduced into the costs imposed, so that different institutions are asked to pay differing amounts. In this case the variable relates to the 'size' of the institution, and deals may be offered in a series of bands (i.e. institutions smaller than X pay Y, institutions greater than X pay Z, etc.) or may be calculated on an individual basis (i.e. size of institution = Q, price of one unit = P, therefore cost is $Q \times P$). The question that arises is how the 'size' of an institution is calculated. Again this can vary from licence to licence, but common figures employed are the numbers of employees or full-time students, the number of machines with potential access to the product, or even the number of ports (i.e. sockets in the wall) available. It is useful if all this information is readily available and kept up to date, so that when necessary a collection developer can get a quick estimate of the cost (e.g. see **http://hul.harvard.edu/digacq/vendors.html**).

Example

A firm has 1000 employees. The licence for a particular dataset is based on a unit access fee of £10 per annum. Therefore the cost of buying the dataset would be £10,000 each year.

Advantages

- There is a sense of equity here as smaller institutions will often pay less.

Disadvantages

- Collecting the figures for 'size' can often be problematic.
- Size does not always equate to 'use', as a smaller institution may make much more use of a product than a larger one.

Payment depends upon a defined and limited set of users

Here the cost is generally established on the understanding that only a certain set of users can access the dataset. For example, the fee may 'buy' 100 individual usernames and passwords which can be issued to the appropriate people, or a few machines can be specified as those enabling access to the product.

Advantages

- It is a set cost that protects, and easily identifies, appropriate users.

Disadvantages

- It is extremely inflexible, restricting access to a particular individual or machine.
- There is an administrative burden involved in identifying the users or machines and issuing passwords, configuring access, and so on. If users leave or machines are replaced this information has to be updated.

Payment depends upon the number of simultaneous users

In this scenario the number of accesses allowed *at the same time* is the defining factor. For example, if an institution has purchased a 'five-simultaneous-user licence' then any authorized user can access the dataset, but if five people are currently using it, a sixth person who attempts to do so will be refused access (until someone logs off). The definition of 'use' needs to be agreed, and there should be a time-out option, so that if a user leaves without logging off, automatic disconnection after a period of time will leave the 'slot' free for the next person.

Advantages

- This allows for an incremental approach to licence purchasing. You can start the deal at a reasonable level and then add extra user slots if demand requires it.
- It is a fixed cost with no variation, unless extra access slots are purchased.
- It is extremely flexible – institutions can tailor their licence according to their needs.

Disadvantages

- The original estimate for the number of simultaneous users is often hard to gauge.
- The desire to minimize costs means there will undoubtedly be 'turn-aways' (users denied access) which can cause ill-feeling: this must be monitored.
- If the dataset is held locally there will be extra work for the IT support staff to make sure this system works.

Payment is transactional (i.e. pay-per-view)

In this scenario payment is based on the number of times the dataset is used. Again the definition of use is problematic as it can be calculated by the number of searches, or the amount of time the user is logged on, or the charge can be levied if the user wishes to print or download any part of the dataset.

Advantages

- Payment is directly linked to use, and thus a dataset that is searched only a handful of times will not cost a large annual fee.
- Budgets can be assigned to individual subdepartments, and thus different sectors in the institution do not feel that they are supporting other sections.

Disadvantages

- The main disadvantage relates to the uncertainty about the eventual financial cost. Certainly at the beginning of the subscription you may have no idea how much use there will be of the dataset, and therefore no idea of the resulting fee. The system is also open to abuse – one person can deliberately or inadvertently incur a high charge for the department.
- Administratively this can also be a problem. A decision will need to be made as to who will actually pay the bill – will the whole institution cover it, will it be divided according to use amongst subdivisions, or will the individual be responsible? Equally important would be the contingency plan should any of the above refuse to pay (or find themselves unable to cover the cost).

The whole situation is complicated even further by the fact that some licences involve a variety of combinations of any of the above. Yet regardless of which payment system is in place, the basic principle is to try to choose a pricing model that will present the best value for money (i.e. financial cost weighed up against the costs of administration and so on). We should now face the question that we side-stepped earlier – what exactly is a fair price? Or to put it another way, how much should people have to pay for a dataset?

Once again, let us remind ourselves of the difficulties faced in answering this. As we noted earlier each institution will have different needs and priorities, and, of course, varying budgets. The 'value' placed on the content of the dataset will subsequently vary, and the datasets themselves are not all equal in terms of size or performance. Prices for datasets will also vary from country to country, and from sector to sector (i.e. educational/non-profit versus commercial). Therefore one cannot state what exactly is a fair price without looking at averages across sectors and countries.

The recommendation of this book therefore is that each institution needs to consider what it thinks is a fair price. This could be calculated by looking at the range of prices for products already subscribed to, and comparing them with their content. For example, in the United Kingdom an educational institution or non–profit-making venture may consider that datasets could be categorized as being essential, useful, or of marginal use. In turn they may wish to band each dataset in terms of possible cost – i.e. a 'fair price' for anything essential may be £10,000, for anything considered 'useful' a ceiling of £5000 may be imposed, and so on. Larger institutions could have higher price ranges (e.g. £30,000 maximum subscription for an essential service), and conversely smaller institutions may have to limit themselves to no more than £5000 on any single product.

Any dataset that could be considered to be in a beta-test stage should have a greatly reduced price. In effect the purchasing institution is being used to provide feedback to the publisher on how good or bad their product is. Although they may be getting access to the data at an earlier stage than if they had waited for the full publication, the fact that it may need fine tuning should be reflected in the price.

The above discussion does not, however, make any reference to hidden costs or more exactly those extra costs that will be incurred by or passed on to the end–user or individual departments. Although it is very easy to simply look at the cost of a dataset in terms of the money required to cover the licence, other factors that should be considered are:

1 cost to network the dataset (or maintain it) if it is held locally
2 any additional software needed or upgrades to operating systems
3 printing costs
4 training courses required or additional user manuals, guides, and so on.

Access restrictions

These naturally follow on from the discussion concerning pricing models, as the various methods (such as limited users, or simultaneous users) will require some form of authentication system to control access. Ideally when negotiating with a publisher there should be minimal access restrictions in order to allow as many legitimate users as required to use the resource regardless of time or geographical constraints. At the same time the concerns of the vendor with reference to security and misuse must be taken into account. For example, a commercial company may need to insist that their workers can access the material from home, whilst travelling abroad, and so on. At the same time the vendor will have to be certain that if international access is granted only legitimate users which would be covered by the company's subscription are admitted. In many ways, then, this will depend upon the authentication issues discussed in Chapter 2.

There should also be a clear statement as to who is classed as an authorized user in the licence. Is this simply members of the subscribing institution, or would it also allow for 'walk-in' users, an issue of particular concern to public libraries? Similarly, what is the exact location that is defined as appropriate (usually referred to as the 'site' in the licence)? Institutions whose premises are distributed, but all form part of the same company, must be protected from having to pay for multiple licences for each separate division.

Equally important, especially when it comes to online subscriptions, is the topic of downtime. The licence should guarantee service availability round the clock, and if maintenance requirements mean this is not possible, compensation for any loss of service, and the procedure for notifying users, should be made clear.

Re-use

The agreement should allow the re-use of material on an equitable basis (i.e. not for resale). This could cover, say, the display of material, but the following should also be allowed:

1   printing
2   saving/copying to disk or other electronic media (but not for republication, of course)
3   archiving the material
4   faxing or e-mailing the data
5   linking to it
6   cacheing
7   making some of the material available via interlibrary loan
8   use on intranets
9   use for educational purposes (i.e. course packs), or scientific research.

Long-term access

This is of considerable concern, and has already been discussed in Chapter 2. The agreement should safeguard long-term access to all the material subscribed to, either by permitting copying for archival purposes, or, should the subscription cease, by allowing the institution to receive copies of all the material made available during the period the licence covered.

File formats

If the publisher agrees to deliver the material (either as part of the usual deal or because of archiving reasons noted above) then the file format becomes important. There are, of course, a multitude of formats (PDF, SGML/XML or plain text, to name but a few in the textual arena), and what is chosen will depend on the services the commercial vendor can offer. Nevertheless, the collection developer should already have a clear view of the range of file formats required and be in a position to request these. For guidance, when dealing with e-journals most people ask for plain text versions (marked up in SGML or XML) when it comes to archiving the material, though PDF offers a good and easy distribution solution.

Integration

Connected with all of the above is the concept of integration. If the material has been purchased then it should be feasible to integrate it with other collections wherever technically possible. If the files are delivered to the local institution then the licence should allow them to be mounted on a server in an integrated environment with other material if so required (i.e. possibly allowing for cross-searching). If the files are held remotely then the publisher should (at the very least) be investigating how their service could be compatible with other similar collections (i.e. using such protocols as Z39.50).

Content and updates

It is essential that the licence spells out exactly what content is included. If this is a replication of printed material it should detail whether the electronic version is an exact replica, or merely a series of abstracts, and so on. How far does the electronic archive extend in terms of back-runs? Is the full bibliographic material available? How often will updates be received, and will they appear prior to any printed edition? A model licence, therefore, would possibly dictate that complete and accurate information is made available as to the electronic product's replication of the printed version, and that a clear timescale for updates is outlined.

Security and anonymity

It should be stated in the licence that any service offered by the publisher (especially when it is a remote service) guarantees security, and above all anonymity for the end-user. Users' searches, results, and analysis must be kept confidential and not passed on (willingly or otherwise) to a third party.

Usage statistics and feedback

These will be discussed in the next chapter, but for the moment the licence to a remote dataset should include an obligation on the part of the publisher to hand over accurate usage statistics in an acceptable format. This is crucial as it will allow the local institution to monitor use (possibly with a view to cancelling the subscription) and to get feedback from their readers. When dealing with remote services this would also include such things as the monitoring of server speeds. Equally important, the publisher should be obliged to meet to discuss this feedback and to act on it wherever possible.

User support

The licence should clearly state how much documentation is available, and what training is on offer. In particular a basic level of help and support should be made available free of charge. A subscriber should not have to pay additionally to find out how to use the product.

Legal issues

In the international world of licences the country under whose laws the agreement is governed should be clearly stated. Products should also adhere to the growing number of guidelines to allow disabled users access to the material (in many countries this is now a legal obligation). Furthermore, the publisher should be required to indemnify the local institution in the case of any misuse of the data which affects a third party.

All of the above does take a very one-sided view of the licence, however. Publishers rightly have rights of their own, and many clauses introduced into the licence which at first may seem unduly restrictive will be there to reflect their legitimate concerns. In particular they will seek to restrict:

1   unauthorized access
2   illegal misuse such as republication, resale, loan, hire, or modification
3   removal of copyright notices.

The model licence is not designed to evade any of these, and it would be wrong to ignore these concerns. Any licence can really only be deemed a success if both parties feel that all their wishes have been addressed.

Ordering the dataset

If we look back at Figure 4.1 we will note that once a satisfactory agreement has been established the next step is to actually order the dataset itself. It is recommended that no money is passed over until the product has been received and, more importantly, has been tested. This is particularly important where there has not been the opportunity to run a trial of the dataset. In this sense then the purchaser should always attempt to avoid payment in advance.

The electronic environment can, of course, facilitate the ordering of such products. Online forms are appearing, and indeed the whole acquisitions process can be assisted in one way or another. As Chapman (2001) states: 'many suppliers now support selection by providing scanned title pages and covers, detailed content descriptions, links to reviews and contents, along with cataloguing data . . . Order records from suppliers can generate MARC cataloguing records, speeding up the processing of new orders' (p. 59). Both electronic collection development and traditional collection development can benefit greatly from this.

Overall management and administrative responsibilities

It should be clear from what we have covered so far that at several steps in the process there is a need to record certain important pieces of information. These are summarized in Table 4.1.

At a glance it is clear that this information will be varied, will come in at different times, and will have direct effects on other decisions. For all these reasons the system chosen has to be flexible, and it should all be readily accessible by any appropriate party. Ideally, therefore, you would wish to have a centralized administrative database system which keeps a track of all evaluations, monitors and adjusts the budget, notifies you well in advance of renewals, and so on. At the very least any form of centralization of the above procedures (if allowable in the local institution) would be of immense benefit in terms of streamlining the whole process. If centralization is impossible, then it is paramount that information is shared as quickly and as comprehensively as possible between the appropriate stakeholders.

Table 4.1   *Stages at which administrative information should be recorded in the life cycle of dataset acquisition*

Stage	Information to be recorded
Awareness of dataset	Details of the dataset
	Details of the proposer
	Date of proposal
Initial assessment and evaluation	All decisions and feedback
Negotiations	All correspondence re the negotiations
Order and payment	Full details of licence
	Any budget alteration
	Any recurrent costs
	Notification to appropriate departments
	Renewal date

Electronic journals (and e-books for that matter) will present an even more complicated situation, bearing in mind the proliferation of titles and bundles, and the importance of hybridity (i.e. maintaining the link between print and electronic subscriptions). In this sense, in addition to the above system, an additional management service might be employed. One such example is TDNet (**www.tdnet.com/**) where the access to, linking, and management of electronic journals is streamlined using an already established database of titles. This also has an effect on delivering the dataset (see the discussions of gateways and cataloguing in Chapter 5).

Chapter summary

In this chapter we have looked at the following:

1   the life cycle of digital collection development
2   the need to formulate a collection development policy
3   establishing a budget
4   finding out about new products
5   evaluations and trials
6   model licences

7   ordering the dataset
8   administering the process.

We now need to complete the life cycle of digital collection development by looking at the delivery of the product.

5 Delivering the dataset

Introduction

In the previous chapter we took a step-by-step approach to the life cycle of electronic collection development. At its conclusion we had reached the stage of having evaluated the product and negotiated the licence, and finally of purchasing the dataset. There are still several stages left to cover after the initial payment of the invoice, as Figure 5.1 shows. We will look at each of these in turn in this chapter, and conclude with a general discussion of how this system might be put to work in an institution.

Cataloguing and delivering the dataset

Once the dataset has been paid for, the priority is to get it out to the users as quickly as possible. Any delay should be seen as a waste, especially if the product is being subscribed to. Figure 5.1 notes that an extra step has to be taken if the product is to be run locally. The dataset must be mounted on the local server (usually an intranet) so that it is available to users, but keeping in mind the terms of licence, as it is important to adhere to any access restrictions imposed. If a trial has not been run already it will be at this point that several problems can arise, such as:

- the product will simply not run across standard networks
- the product will network but requires additional work at the client end – i.e. downloading a piece of software, or mapping a drive for the product to write to
- the product does run on a network but only at a very slow rate, or requires a high-specification machine at the client end to be usable.

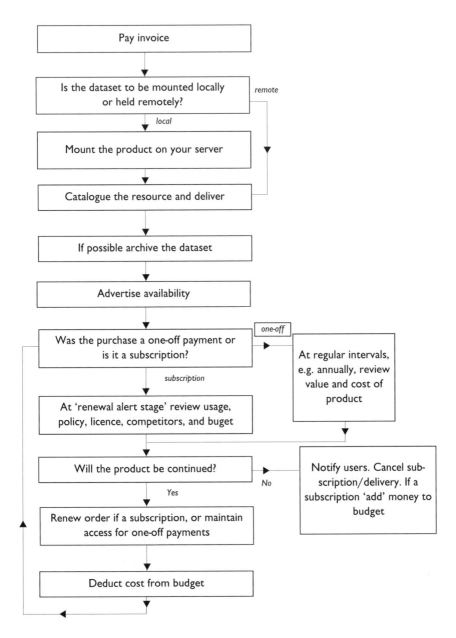

Fig. 5.1   *Secondary stages in dataset acquisition*

The costs involved for overcoming any of the above should not be underestimated. Indeed if you are adopting a holistic stance to collection development then these additional costs should possibly be reflected in a change in the budget. Again this information should be noted in whatever central administration system is set up (as advocated at the end of the last chapter).

Assuming that the dataset is available, either remotely or locally, it needs to be integrated into some system by which the reader can easily find it and access it. There are a variety of ways of doing this and anything that is accessible via the web, of course, can be linked to from anywhere with appropriate privileges (see Xie and Cool, 2000, for a further analysis of this). For example, subdivisions within the institution may run their own websites but might wish to link directly to the online resource. This, though, can cause problems. First it is generally the case that when left to their own devices smaller sections tend to provide very little extra information about the resource, not just with reference to the content but also to the technical issues the user may need to think about before accessing it. Second, especially in the case of remote services, website addresses have a tendency to change. As soon as they do, all of the individual pages that link directly to the resource will have to be modified.

For these reasons (and others) most institutions that build up a collection of electronic resources tend to provide a central catalogue which, wherever possible, also acts as a means of direct access. Subdivisions within the institution can then link to this catalogue (or the appropriate entry in it). Whichever body is responsible for maintaining this, however, will also be charged with providing all the extra information required. This is clearly more efficient. In the example above, if a URL changes then only the entry on the single catalogue needs to be altered, not a series of individual pages.

This forms the basis of the following discussion (but we should note that many of the issues touched on are common to cataloguing any electronic material, such as websites). There are two approaches to cataloguing which are often adopted: a gateway, or integration with existing catalogues. In a sense the former segregates electronic resources from the main collections, whilst the latter attempts to streamline all the holdings.

A gateway catalogue

A gateway, or hub, is simply an index of all the electronic resources available. The term can be used to cover a variety of concepts, ranging from a local institution's attempt to bring together its electronic resources into a meaningful whole, to the large web 'catalogues' run by such companies as Yahoo! or the W3C. For the purposes of this book we are interested in the former.

If all the resources to be catalogued are internet-based, then a gateway might simply mean an HTML webpage listing all of the products in alphabetical order. This will be complicated, of course, if the collection is typical in that it mixes remote and locally held resources. The latter, usually produced on CD-ROM for a Windows platform, will have to be mounted on some form of local server (as noted above), which will depend entirely on the specifications of the publisher. A simple webpage will probably not suffice, as the client will need access to a Windows search interface, and possibly some additional software. Clearly this is not ideal as it would be difficult to make this available outside of an intranet, and above all to readers working on different platforms (such as Macintosh or UNIX machines). Solutions do exist for some products (such as those that are SilverPlatter-compliant, as noted in Chapter 2), but again this would require extra support (and hence extra costs).

There are also issues of interface design that need to be faced. How can the gateway be made to be intuitive, easy to navigate, and as comprehensive as possible? Some answers are suggested in the following collation of the types of features and sections that are commonly available on gateways to electronic resources.

1   *Subject index and title index.* Here the user is presented with one of two options (or both if possible) to allow access to the titles. Grouping products into different subject areas (for example this might be individual disciplines in a university or sections in a company) might

be a good way to present choices to the new user, especially if there are a lot of resources (some of which will have non-intuitive titles). As always, though, problems of taxonomy will arise soon, so for this to work successfully you may need to duplicate some listings (where products are interdisciplinary in nature) and above all seek guidance from the subject experts. Particular problems arise with e-journals where bundles of products will cover all ranges of subjects. To avoid this you could consider presenting a generic subject heading such as 'Online journals'. You should also provide an alphabetical index of all the titles in the collection so that users have a better chance of finding a specific title more quickly.

2 *Intermediary step.* Once a title has been found it is commonplace to insert an intermediary screen, or explanatory section (held locally as opposed to the product's own 'introduction'), before the user actually accesses the dataset. This will serve two purposes: first, it will limit the chances of the user accidentally selecting the wrong title. Second, it presents an opportunity to give the reader more information on the scope of the product (especially useful with 'umbrella' titles), and to inform them of any third-party software they will need, usernames or passwords required, other authentication systems in place, and so on.

3 *Search facility.* Although we will look at cataloguing in more detail later on, it is worth noting that many gateways will provide the reader with a search facility to assist them in locating a specific resource. Ideally this would contain lengthier descriptions and keywords to direct them to products that, by their title, may not seem directly relevant to their needs. However, even allowing for a search simply on the title itself will assist some users, especially when confronted with a large dataset.

4 *Cross-search facility.* Although we have been concentrating on titles as individual products, it is becoming possible to cross-search different products at the same time. This will inherently depend upon the product itself and what protocols or platforms it supports, but the user should be made aware if this is an option. Similarly, if users have the option to cross-search several titles they should be allowed to select subsets if possible.

5 *Downloads and configurations.* We have noted that at the intermediary step you can include information on any peculiarities in terms of configurations that the individual product may require. It is also useful to try to collate this information into a single section, so that anyone supporting a client machine (whether a technician or a user) can have immediate access to all the downloads and configurations they will need to perform to allow an individual machine to access all the products.

6 *Latest acquisitions and trials.* Although you may have sent out notifications of new products or ongoing evaluations already, it is worth listing these on the gateway in a single section. There is a reasonable chance, then, that any user who missed the circular will encounter new items via this route.

7 *Troubleshooting and FAQs.* It is standard practice to provide information on common problems and frequently asked questions, covering such things as problems with configurations, how to access remote datasets, problems encountered with authentication systems, and so on.

8 *Links to policy statements.* In Chapter 4 it was suggested that a policy statement (or a genre statement) should be drawn up outlining the major policy issues and decisions. This should be included in the gateway or linked to as appropriate.

9 *User profiles.* As systems become more advanced, the ability to personalize a gateway may be offered. Here superfluous titles could be omitted, and only those of direct relevance to the user might be listed.

10 *Feedback.* It is clear, however, that even with all the above in place not all the questions that users might ask will be immediately answered. Therefore it is essential that there is some way for them to make comments, suggestions, and criticisms. This could also operate in tandem with a means of suggesting new titles (if the institution's policy allows for such a thing).

Integration with existing catalogues

There are two problems with the gateway approach (if left by itself). First, it clearly goes against the proposition that electronic resource collection should be seen as part of, and not separate from, traditional collection development. In other words, although a gateway may link to online catalogues of print holdings, the impression may be given that print and electronic are still distinct from each other rather than complementary. Second, because of the way most users operate, their traditional access point to collections will usually be the standard library catalogue – the OPAC. How will the items listed on the gateway come to their attention if they do not veer from this course?

The gateway approach is very common, though, mainly because historically it provided a way of keeping an eye on this new area of collection development without losing sight of it amidst the larger print collections. It also serves to alert users to the new world of electronic resources, again without swamping them with traditional collections. This is still a valid concern in many institutions, and the total abandonment of the gateway approach is not advocated here. Yet, at the same time, we must consider how electronic resources can be listed in the traditional online library catalogue.

When we look at cataloguing in this sense it is advisable to clarify exactly what we are attempting to do. In short, the cataloguing of electronic resources should:

1 reflect the wishes and requirements of as many of the stakeholders as possible (listed later)
2 assist readers in locating and accessing material
3 help collection managers to keep a track of availability
4 provide all the information that IT specialists wish to know or wish to make available.

In many ways then we are replicating the functions already served by existing cataloguing systems. It is extremely important to remember that the systems and solutions noted below are being developed to achieve the above worthy objectives, and much of the work is being carried out by librarians who would see all of the above as valid in both arenas (print or digital). In this light it is not surprising that traditional systems, such as

MARC, are being used in an attempt to catalogue electronic resources. We might envisage a scenario whereby the user searching the OPAC will locate electronic as well as print resources.

Before looking at this in more detail it is worth noting that cataloguing systems have also emerged from the digital world. These, in general, have focused on the cataloguing of internet resources such as websites. A very common standard adopted is the Dublin Core Metadata Initiative. Although this may not be of use to everyone wishing to catalogue their electronic resources as part of an existing OPAC, it is useful to look at the areas the Dublin Core prioritizes. An interesting adaptation is that of the UK's Humbul Humanities Hub (part of the Resource Discovery Network, **www.humbul.ac.uk/**), which seeks to catalogue resources on a national scale. In this version of the Dublin Core the headings include:

1   Title of the resource (plus any alternative titles)
2   Location, i.e. URL
3   Responsibility (name of author(s), their role(s) and affiliation(s))
4   Contact details for the person or institution responsible for the resource
5   Publisher or other distributor(s) of the resource (again with information such as the name and role of a main contact, with affiliation and other details)
6   Description of the content of the resource itself
7   Main language the resource is presented in (e.g. French, Spanish, etc.)
8   Type of the resource (e.g. courseware, bibliographic source, etc.).

This is not a definitive list, but it does illustrate some of the issues that need to be accommodated in traditional cataloguing systems if they are to cope with electronic resources.

Important work in this area is being performed by the joint steering committee for the revision of the Anglo-American Cataloguing Rules (AACR2). A general overview is available under the Library of Congress's *Bicentennial Conference on Bibliographic Control for the New Millennium* (**http://lcWeb.loc.gov/catdir/bibcontrol/**, with a full description at

www.nlc–bnc.ca/jsc/). Other initiatives that should also be noted include the *International standard bibliographic description for electronic resources* (**http://ifla.inist.fr/VII/s13/pubs/isbd.htm**), the Library of Congress's *Draft interim guidelines for cataloging electronic resources* (**http://lcweb.loc.gov/ catdir/cpso/elec_res.html**), Oxford University's *Cataloguing electronic resources* (**www.bodley.ox.ac.uk/dept/techserv/ulstst/catsig/docs/ eresources/cataloguing.pdf**), or the exemplary work of J. Weitz and N. Olson for OCLC (plus the CORC initiative – **www.oclc.org/corc/**). Readers will also find the studies by Hsieh–Yee (2000) and Weihs (1991) of help. Here we need present only a summary of the main issues that people will encounter. For more detailed explanations, such as particular MARC fields or the final revision of AACR2, readers are referred to the above.

What emerging issues, then, can we abstract from the above? In some cases solutions are already on offer, but elsewhere discussion is still ongoing. It is perhaps best to look at the following, then, only as a preliminary list of the problems that may be encountered when attempting to catalogue electronic resources using traditional systems. Although at times reference is made to AACR2/MARC, the problems are common to all cataloguing standards:

1   *Identifying the type of resource*. The generic description of a resource as a 'computer file' used in the past quite liberally (i.e. type code 'm' in MARC) does not convey its true meaning, and thus fails one of the main aims of cataloguing – to inform the user. How do we distinguish between a resource that is mainly textual in its content as opposed to numerical? How do we catalogue games or other software? How do we distinguish between a locally held resource and a remote service? The distinction between type code 'a' (language material) and 'm' in the 'type of record' field in MARC now allows for this in part, as does the special material designation 'r' for 'remote' in the 'physical description' field. The general material designation (GMD) in MARC will also allow, for example, the distinguishing entry 'electronic resource' which may be useful when it comes to parallel print publications.

2 *Is the product to be classed as a monograph or serial?* In the case of a standalone title (such as a one-off CD-ROM) this is not an issue, but many products are consistently updated, especially internet-based resources. How can the catalogue effectively reflect this? Should the product be considered a serial? The answer perhaps lies in the significance of the update, and its regularity. Most systems would catalogue such resources as A&I services, OPACs, databases, and similar as monographs, reserving the serial classification for products where complete designated parts are updated, or where there is an entire replacement pattern.

3 *Which part of a resource is to be catalogued?* This is a particular issue when it comes to internet sites, where subsections of the site may be of more interest to specific users and thus deserve separate indexing. How do we decide which level in the hierarchy of the site deserves a bibliographic record? Again this rests on knowledge of user expectations. If a particular subsection of a site can be identified as something a user would search for (which is not intuitive in the title for the whole site) then it warrants its own entry (as well as one, perhaps, for the entire site itself).

4 *When and where was a resource created, and when does it become a new resource?* Publication information, including the 'physical' location of an internet site, is often very difficult to ascertain, though such information is generally required by traditional cataloguing systems. If the information is unknown, then this should be indicated. If it is open-ended then that should also be stated (e.g. 2000 onwards). Even more difficult is the problem of when a resource should be considered a new resource, i.e. a new 'edition'. This ties in with the observations about monographs and serials above, but in short it is often a matter of discretion. If the resource appears to have undergone only minor changes then it should not be considered a new edition. However, if there have been wholesale changes and alterations then it could be considered as such.

5 *What is the difference between a reproduction and a republication?* For cataloguing purposes an electronic resource should generally be listed as a reproduction if it is meant as a substitute for the original (i.e. a

scanned facsimile). If it is meant to be a complementary publication then it should be considered a republication.

6   *How is information about system requirements conveyed?* As we have noted throughout this book, additional information will be required on all the downloads and configurations needed, and the location (e.g. the URL) and so on of the electronic resource. In other words, the catalogue will have to cope with this new type of information ('new' as it is not often apparent in print publications). System requirements therefore should be noted (such as the need for third-party software), plus the mode of access (MARC field 538, for example), as well as authentication procedures required ('restriction to access' in MARC field 506). There are also a variety of ways of accessing or receiving material, as we have noted throughout this book, and again this should be recorded in the catalogue entry (e.g. it should be clear whether a journal is e-mailed to the recipient, made available via FTP, or, as is increasingly the case, is online via the web).

7   *How should e-journals and e-books be approached?* There are particular issues which arise when dealing with these two products, but for the moment at least (understandably so, if one reflects on the chronology of their development) most work has centred on e-journals. If the electronic journal to be catalogued is a complete version of the print publication then it is recommended that a separate bibliographic entry is made for each with some form of linking between the two. For the print version entry the availability of the e-version should be noted, any differences between the two, a link to the e-journal, and an indication of its 'virtual' location. Similar information should be available in the bibliographic record for the e-version. It is important to get the information as exact as possible, especially noting the pitfalls involved in title changes when a product moves from print to electronic. However minor these may seem at first they must be recorded accurately. If the titles are the same you may wish to include a reference such as 'online version' to distinguish between print and electronic. The authority of the title should also be noted – is it being taken from the opening page or screen? Or is it a personal customization? – and so on. An e-journal may have an ISSN, which

should be noted (N.B. this will not be the same as the ISSN for the print journal).

There are other issues which are discussed at length in the previously mentioned studies, but this short list gives an impression of what problems are currently being targeted, and in some cases the solutions that are on offer. The main reason for putting effort into adapting existing cataloguing systems is to allow the user to find the electronic resource more readily. In other words, if the OPAC can be adapted so that it can record such information, overcoming the issues raised above, and then link directly to the resource itself, this will greatly supplement (and possible negate the need for) the gateway approach discussed earlier.

We should also note that the problems confronting metadata standards above (that is to say cataloguing information, or data about the data itself) could also arise in a more complicated gateway approach (i.e. it is perfectly feasible to use AACR2/MARC to build a gateway of electronic resources). Again we return to our earlier observation that the gateway, if adopted, would tend to segregate electronic resources from mainstream holdings, whilst a general catalogue for all material would tend towards integration. We need to ask what would be the most useful to the readers? Do not be surprised if the answer is 'both'. This awareness of the needs of the users, or the function the catalogue intends to serve, will also influence the type of information recorded and its level of complexity. The context of the catalogue is everything. To use our example of HUMBUL earlier, cataloguers are asked to 'describe resources with a mixture of factual information and value judgements' (collection development policy, 3.2). This is entirely valid for such an open resource used by disparate communities. However, if the catalogue is much more focused, as in attempting to serve the needs of a local OPAC for identified readers, 'value judgements' may not be appropriate.

Archiving the dataset

The next step, once the dataset is classed as being 'available', is to archive the product (if the data is held locally in some form). This can be done at any time in the process from the initial receipt of the product right up to its announcement, but, for safety reasons, the sooner the better. When dealing with large quantities of data, a high-storage secure back-up service is needed, and wherever possible the data should be exported to a non-proprietary standard also. This will never give a cast-iron guarantee that in the future the dataset will be accessible (that is to say with all its original functionality) but it is the best option. Remotely held datasets are problematic, of course, and a lot will depend on the terms of the licence. Some agreements will state that the publisher is obligated to supply a copy of the data, whilst others will detail that they or a third party will guarantee remote long-term access to the product up to the point of the last subscription. Some, alas, will guarantee neither of these.

Advertising the dataset

As soon as the dataset is delivered and available via whatever interface is offered, all the stakeholders should be notified quickly. It is clearly sensible to get people using the products as soon as possible (and consequently initiating feedback), as any delay, especially with a subscription service, is a waste of time and money. As noted earlier it is also advisable to maintain a central list of recently purchased datasets for those who may have missed any circulars.

Activities post-purchasing

So far so good. The product has now been evaluated, purchased, and made available, and the users have been notified. Yet even now the whole process does not come to an end. The term 'life cycle' used in Chapter 4 was chosen specifically to make it clear that this is a continual process. Even if a product is a one-off purchase (i.e. not a subscription) it will still need to be monitored and reviewed at a later stage.

Figure 5.1 outlines the next steps in the process. It is suggested that there is a division at this point between products that are running under a subscription, and those that were one-off payments in the first place. Yet the final decision to be made is the same, namely: should the service be continued or not? When it comes to one-off purchases many are misled into believing that this is not really an issue as no further money is being requested. Yet it is important to review these products nevertheless. Every networked product will incur a cost, however marginal, including such things as maintaining the product, maintaining the server that is needed to house the product, or the value of the space on the server it may be occupying (assuming it is a locally mounted product). That is to say, discontinuation of a product, i.e. not offering it to users any more, may result in a saving in terms of the burden on the support staff, freeing up space on the server, and so on.

Clayton and Gorman (2001, 203) note the following reasons for deselecting (as they term it) electronic media:

- expenditure
- the product has been duplicated or superseded by more recent material
- the product is hard to use
- changing hardware/software requirements.

All of these are clearly valid. So, how might we go about deselecting an item?

If we follow the diagram, it is noted that for one-off purchases these should be checked at regular intervals. There is no set definition of what such an interval might be, but probably an annual review may be satisfactory for most institutions. At this point the cost of the product (including all of the 'hidden' costs noted above) should be weighed against its value to the readers. For a subscription service it is recommended that a 'renewal alert stage' is established for every product. This could be three months prior to the time when the subscription will need to be renewed, to allow plenty of time to assess the licence, to see if any competitors have come onto the market which present a more attractive alternative, and to analyse the state of play of the next budget. Notably with the latter it would be ideal if any decisions to renew a subscription could coincide with the calculations for the next budget. It should be remembered that some deals have an initial commitment period (i.e. tying the customer into the deal for a period at the beginning of the subscription for anything between two and five years). Yet this will usually revert to an annual subscription after that, so again a renewal alerting stage could be established in the final quarter of the subscription.

Unfortunately, as products and deals emerge throughout the year, renewal periods will undoubtedly become staggered, and thus the process will have to be monitored for the whole twelve months. It is true that there will be a cluster of deals around the end of the financial year (in the commercial sector) or the academic year (in the educational sector), but there will also be several subscriptions that will need attention at other periods.

Usage statistics

When attempting to value a dataset in terms of its importance to readers, we inevitably fall back on usage statistics as the most tangible way of measuring its worth. To put it crudely, if the product is being used a lot then it must be of value. This is a very blunt tool to attempt to value such a nebulous concept, and there are many caveats which should be considered when using such means. For example, the statistics may reveal that only a handful of employees are using a product and only for a few times a month. Yet without interviewing the users this will not reveal the value of the information they derived from the dataset – it may well be that the information was crucial to securing a deal or finding out about key areas of the market, and without access to that resource the company might have lost money elsewhere. Low use may also be due to technical problems with the product, which if overcome may mean that it is accessed much more. Or it could simply be that the readers are not aware of the resource yet and further advertising is needed. On the other hand, a review of the statistics may indicate that although a dataset is being accessed several times a day by a lot of people, they only use it for a minute or so, thus indicating that once they are into the resource they realize it is of very little use.

In short, then, although usage statistics are informative to an extent they should be employed in conjunction with other forms of analysis. A quick informal survey of the most likely users of a product at the renewal stage might give a more accurate reflection of the dataset's actual worth. Nevertheless, what information can we expect usage statistics to yield? A comprehensive list is available in the UK's JISC initial discussion document on 'Vendor based usage statistics collection' (**www. jisc.ac. uk/curriss/collab/c6_pub/uswg/**). However, for a general guide readers might wish to consider the following:

1   *Accurate delineation.* The statistics must be clear as to what they are referring to. For example, an umbrella product by definition contains several titles: it is clear that you would wish to be able to distinguish use by each specific dataset, and in the case of e-journals by each journal title and maybe even down to the article level.

2   *Session details.* At the client end you will also want to be able to clearly see use by any separate divisions in the local institution, and possibly even by individual machines or users (i.e. via IP addresses or usernames and passwords). You will want accurate information on exactly when the searches are made (the time *and* the date are preferable), and the sessions for each user (again such things as the time the reader was logged on, the number of queries per session, and similar are required). Failed sessions, or as they were termed earlier, 'turn-aways', should also be recorded (distinguishing between those that failed for reasons of too many concurrent accesses and those that failed for other reasons). This information is vital if you are to reassess the subscription. User confidentiality, though, as always, has to be maintained throughout: that is to say details about the session, and the user's interaction with the product, should not be given to third parties without the user's consent.

3   *Details of queries.* Full details about the user's interaction with the dataset should be given (as completely as possible). Information on the number of searches, the resulting hits that were followed up and examined, the number of browses, and so on, should all be presented. As noted above, with subtitles in an umbrella product these figures should be tied to particular datasets so that an overall impression of the granularity of use can be observed (by 'granularity' we mean fine-

tuning the usage statistics as that use of individual titles and sections by readers can be identified). Information should be available on what the user then did with the results, i.e. were they e-mailed, downloaded, and so on.

4   *Comparative statistics.* Figures on the level of use at other comparable institutions would also be valuable, as it would indicate whether there might be a need to reassess the training offered to users or to re-advertise the product. At the same time though, institutional confidentiality needs to be maintained, especially in the competitive commercial sector.

If the dataset is held locally it is up to the host institution to derive these statistics. If it is held remotely then the publisher or supplier should be obliged to pass these on, if the guidelines of the model licence in the previous chapter have been followed. Atherton (2001) noted that at present 47% of publishers provide usage statistic data, and 29% of those who currently do not, plan to. In other words, in a very short time the majority of electronic publishers will be supplying their subscribers with data. Indeed from the publisher's perspective statistics are extremely important when trying to monitor such things as excessive downloads which may indicate illegal use. It is important to note at this point that in order to get as true a picture as possible, wherever feasible the data should be sought directly from the publisher, and not from any third party (i.e. an aggregator).

Yet what exactly will all these figures tell you? Bearing in mind the caveats noted earlier about the fallibility of such figures, how can they be effectively utilized? One suggestion would be to look at the returns from all the datasets and try to establish levels of use. Some products will illustrate very high levels of use, and it may be clear from existing knowledge of the local readers that this is a true reflection of the dataset's importance. Then there will be products that are used reasonably frequently, and some that are hardly ever used. An 'average use per day' figure might be a good way to proceed at this point. Once this has been established across all the datasets it will be obvious which titles have an extremely low use compared with the average. On a regular basis these figures could be reviewed, and then those that were perceived to be below any acceptable level of use could be investigated further. Note that it is not an automatic decision to cancel the product at this point, but more a signal for further study to be initiated as to why the usage might be so low.

The decision to cancel or renew

The purpose of the analysis undertaken so far has been to review the subscription, or the value of maintaining access to an already owned dataset. The outcome of such an analysis will basically come down to one of three options:

- cancel the product (i.e. cancel the subscription or remove the owned dataset from the network)
- maintain access to the product (i.e. renew the subscription or simply keep a locally owned dataset on the server)
- maintain access with modifications.

We have already looked at why either of the first two might be chosen; 'modifications' in the third category can mean such things as increasing simultaneous user access, or indeed any alteration to the licence to reflect user demands. With the exception of a few fossilized titles the decision to cancel a dataset or to alter the access restrictions in any way that might have a detrimental effect on its use should not be taken lightly. Any cancellation, in particular, should only be done after wide consultation with the readers, unless it is simply unavoidable for financial reasons. Even then the users should be told as quickly and as fully as possible about the decision.

Above all you must be certain about the decision, and have confidence that all mitigating circumstances have been explored and possible repercussions anticipated. For example, if you base the decision to cancel on low usage statistics then it should be shown that (a) the statistics accurately represent true use of the product, and (b) there were no other reasons that may have affected the statistics. Examples of the latter might include poor advertising or teething problems with the initial installation. Even when cancelling a title and replacing it with a competitive service the situation is not as straightforward as it may seem. Although the switch to the new service may have been made on the grounds that it is cheaper and thus represents a direct cost-cutting exercise, the hidden costs of moving a large body of users from one service to another must be taken into account (i.e. training, administering new authentication systems, and so on).

Nevertheless, whatever decision is made will have a direct effect on both the budget and the overall collection development strategy of the institution. It may immediately represent a cost saving, an increased expenditure, or no alteration. Any stakeholders that are affected by the decision should be informed as quickly as possible.

The stakeholders

We have frequently mentioned the stakeholders that need to be consulted and informed at various stages. Who exactly are they, or what do they represent? In short, a stakeholder is anyone who is either directly affected by a collection development decision, or would have appropriate input to make which might affect that decision. In other words the relationship between collection development and stakeholders should be seen as a two-way process. Figure 5.2 shows the people or sections who could be involved in electronic collection development and (below) the aspects of the infrastructure most directly affected by any decision (the latter being the established budget, which will change throughout the year, and the rest of the collection development activities at the institution). Traditional activities will more than likely draw on the same budget as electronic acquisitions, and thus are directly affected by them.

The upper part of Figure 5.2 shows the people who will be involved in collection-development decisions or contribute to the overall pool of expertise:

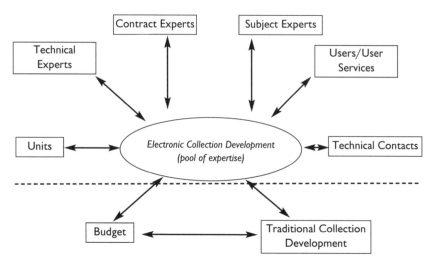

Fig. 5.2   *The stakeholders in dataset acquisition*

- Units: this means any units, subdepartments, faculties, and so on in the institution that might have an interest in the acquisition of electronic resources.
- Technical experts: those who will be asked to network the product, maintain client machines, manage authentication systems, and so on.
- Contract experts: those called upon to help out with licence agreements and rights issues.
- Subject experts: those having expertise in the content of the product or products.
- Users/user services (or reader services): the users or readers themselves, and any other bodies charged with representing, supporting, and training them.
- Technical contacts: nominated individuals whose contact details are given to a publisher on completion of a licence agreement. In this context 'technical' also covers updates, subscription renewals, and so on. It is worth spending some time and effort to draw up a list of all of these people and to maintain it centrally (see Harvard University's 'resource stewards' list, **http://hul.harvard.edu/ digacq/stewards. html**).

In many institutions, be they commercial or academic, the functions and responsibilities outlined above will not fall into such neat categories. For example, it is often the case that many of the duties referred to here may be covered by one or two individuals. This, of course, has great benefits in terms of centralized expertise and the ability to make quick decisions, but can often lead to an excessive amount of work. Nevertheless, it is notable that many libraries nowadays try to recruit a single (and thus 'central') electronic collections development manager who would be in overall charge. Yet even then it is doubtful that he or she would be an expert in all subject areas, or have both legal and technical expertise. Therefore, although there may be a single person responsible for co-ordinating these activities, they will still have to liaise effectively with several other stakeholders.

The user's perspective

Throughout this book we have taken the stance of the collection developer, with only occasional glances to the user (in terms of interface discussions, need for notification, and so on). Yet we have noted above in our discussion of stakeholders that their input is invaluable, and indeed they often have the most to gain or lose from any decision made. It is now time to remedy the balance to some degree and look at how users might wish to approach a collection of electronic resources.

Exactly how and why users interact with datasets is being explored at the moment by a UK project entitled JUSTEIS (JISC Usage Surveys: Trends in Electronic Information Services). At the moment only a preliminary report on their findings has been released (**www.dil.aber.ac.uk/dils/Research/JUSTEIS/cyc1rep0.htm**), but the site is worth monitoring. In terms of our general observations it is clear that the main activity readers perform is to try to find information that will be of use to them (in their work). To put this more concretely: users interact with datasets for research purposes (commercial or academic) or for training and teaching.

Teaching with datasets

The networked resources on offer in many institutions present a wonderful asset to the trainer or teacher. Most notably the material lends itself well to resource-based learning as it allows people access to a wealth of information otherwise unavailable (or in a less easy format to search). However, the flipside to this is that the number of products and their coverage can overwhelm users who may feel swamped by the number of choices at their disposal, and somewhat disillusioned if their initial searches return thousands upon thousands of hits. Yet it is also clear that many teachers or instructors want to make use of these resources in their courses. How can this be achieved without the reader's becoming disillusioned? The following is an initial list of practical suggestions:

- The most obvious place for the inclusion of networked resources is in the reading list for the course. It is important to be selective in the material to which the students are directed. It is not advisable to simply issue instructions on how to access a gateway (for example) or the generic catalogue, but rather point to specific titles or services, or selected topics within them.
- If a particular resource is directly applicable to a course, then (depending upon the facilities available) an interactive session, involving supervised searching and browsing of the dataset, could form a class in itself.
- If the delegates attending the course are complete novices at using computers it may be worthwhile arranging for some preliminary training.
- It is worth instructing users on how to conduct their searches more effectively. They should, for example, be encouraged to look at the advanced search features, and find out how to save or e-mail results back to themselves.
- Be reasonably versed in the functionality and contents of each of the titles selected.
- Be aware of the facilities at all the locations from where the readers will be accessing the products, and the difficulties that may arise locally. It is perhaps worthwhile checking with them early on to see if

they are experiencing any problems in getting access to the products.

- If you wish to use the resources in the training room itself, then, outside of small-group teaching, you will need a computer that can connect to the dataset, a projection unit, and a projection screen. It is strongly advised that before the course starts someone checks that everything is working, especially access to the products. To be certain of avoiding any problems, screen shots of various searches could be used, but then you lose the effect of showing dynamic interaction.

Research strategies

In Chapter 2 we outlined the landscape of the dataset. It was clear that the vast array of products would be of great assistance to the researcher, whether commercial or academic. As before, however, for many researchers experienced in traditional methods this immediate access to such a vast amount of resources can prove daunting.

Let us consider how researchers might approach the variety of electronic resources outlined in Chapters 2 and 3:

- They discover material via A&I services, specialist bibliographies, gateways, and other library catalogues.
- They physically locate the desired material in the catalogues of the holders of the data (most commonly OPACs).
- They get access to the actual data (as opposed to its bibliographic reference) via a variety of means. Electronically this might be facilitated by linkage services, online ordering, ILLs, printing, and so on. Traditionally the user would retrieve a physical copy of the material from the library shelf.

In short, users discover, locate, and access. Bearing this in mind, how can they be guided through the process? The following step-by-step approach is offered as a starting set of guidelines:

- Users need to be clear about their research topic. For most of the services available they will need to enter a search term (i.e. a word or phrase). Therefore it is worth taking a few moments to list the various searches they might wish to use.

- If the institution offers a gateway to the resources you could begin by homing in on any subject-specific sections. However, it should be remembered that more often than not any taxonomy, if employed, is never failsafe, and users may need to browse in any sections that have potential overlap.
- The next step is to try to find articles or books published in the area of research. Users should now concentrate on any service (be it a textbase, e-book or e-journal collection) that will allow them to locate a resource and bring it directly to their screen (i.e. it has direct access to the full text).
- Next they should look to the A&I services and other bibliographies. A good starting point would be the appropriate subject-specific bibliographies, from where they could move to larger services such as ISI's Web of Science, OCLC FirstSearch, etc.
- These will point the researcher to a particular article or book, but he or she will then need to use a library catalogue (an OPAC) to find the physical location of the required book or journal. However, it should not be forgotten that library catalogues are also a major research resource in that they too will allow the user to look for books and journals that may be of interest. The user should be directed initially to the local OPAC, and then move to national and international catalogues (possibly using ILL facilities).
- Finally users can begin to move away from the local gateways and intranets and start to use the web, searching the free resources available there. However, it is important that users are advised to always check on the authority of any site visited in terms of its currency and above all its accuracy.

At some point researchers will encounter the problem of how they should actually cite sections of the electronic resources they are using. Although there are no definitive guidelines which are universally accepted the following are good starting points:

- the International Organization for Standardization, *Bibliographic references to electronic documents* (**www.nlc-bnc.ca/iso/tc46sc9/ standard/690-2e.htm**)
- MLA, *How do I document sources from the world wide web?* (**www.mla.org/** – click on 'MLA style', then 'Frequently asked questions about MLA style', then the link to *How do I document sources*)
- Columbia University Press, *Basic CGOS style* (**www.columbia. edu/cu/cup/cgos/idx_basic.html**).

Electronic collection development by numbers

Our overview of electronic collection development is beginning to draw to a close. We will finish this with a step-by-step approach to what, however daunting it may seem at the outset, can be achieved, and how to go about it. In effect what follows is a summary of many of the previous discussions.

1 Get to know your institution

1 Begin by identifying all the stakeholders, i.e. those who are interested in, or affected by, collection development.
2 Try to locate a spokesperson for each group of stakeholders and establish a workable model by which all stakeholders will be able to provide input, or at least could collaborate where centralization is difficult.

2 Get to know your current holdings

1 Survey (possibly via questionnaires) and collate all current collection development policies.
2 Familiarize yourself with the range of products available on the market, as outlined in Chapters 2 and 3.
3 Identify all the electronic titles that have already been purchased or subscribed to (i.e. perform an audit and stocktake of your holdings). If possible create a central repository of licences already

in play. Furthermore, the list of stakeholders can now be supplemented by adding the 'technical contacts' (Chapter 5) for existing products. At the same time, begin to build up a desiderata list of titles people would like to see.

3 Essential administration

1   Formulate some basic selection criteria for datasets (to be refined later) and do an initial run-through of the preliminary desiderata list.
2   Establish a preliminary budget using the guidelines set out in Chapter 4, based on this desiderata list.
3   With the aid of the stakeholders formulate a collection development statement (or genre statement), complete with details about your institution (number of employees or FTEs, facilities, dispersal of units, and so on), and publish this as widely as possible. Further refine your basic criteria for selection and evaluation of products at this point.
4   As part of this, and again using the guidelines in Chapter 4, establish a model licence for your institution. Make this available (e.g. on a website) so that publishers will be able to see the basic ground rules for negotiating.
5   Build or purchase an administrative system to cope with all of the stages noted in Chapter 4.
6   Set up a dissemination scheme to notify stakeholders: e.g. e-mail lists, bulletin boards, a website, training sessions, and print publications.

4 Progressing

1   Start to target titles on the desiderata list for an initial evaluation.
2   Using the criteria in Chapter 4 begin to evaluate the products, bringing in all the appropriate stakeholders.
3   Choose a selection of titles.
4   Identify and order any necessary hardware or software needed to allow access to the chosen titles.

5   Purchase and network titles accordingly and adjust the budget.

6   Flag, for each product, a renewal alerting stage as discussed earlier in this chapter.

7   Archive the products accordingly.

5 Delivering the products

1   Begin with a simple gateway building up a title list, and breaking it down into subject areas (if applicable).

2   Investigate other ways of cataloguing the products via more traditional methods (e.g. integrate the list with your OPAC).

3   Advertise the availability of all the products and initiate any authentication systems needed.

6 Completing the circle

1   Set up a system (e.g. a simple web form) to allow people to nominate new titles. Feed this into your administration system so that the desiderata list is fluid and up to date.

2   At regular intervals assemble the stakeholders (or representatives) to assess the growing desiderata list in terms of your selection criteria noted above.

3   If the budget allows, maintain a cycle of new purchases, and at the same time analyse usage statistics for possible cancellations (at the renewal alerting stage).

4   After the first annual cycle you should be in a position to:
   • establish a more informed budget
   • maintain a responsive desiderata list
   • seamlessly link electronic collection development with traditional collections
   • operate an effective two-way process with all stakeholders
   • catalogue, deliver, and archive all resources purchased.

Chapter summary

In this final chapter we have outlined the remaining stages of the life cycle of electronic collection development. We have taken the process through cataloguing, archiving, and advertising. We have also looked at the steps that should be taken after a dataset has been purchased, including monitoring the use of the product and how to decide on whether to cancel or renew the subscription. The user's perspective has also been looked at, in terms of using datasets in teaching or research. Finally we have proposed a model step-by-step approach to starting off an electronic collection from scratch.

Select glossary

Because many of the terms surrounding the acquisition of datasets are new, or are at least unfamiliar, the following glossary is an attempt to define some of the problematic ones. Readers should note that these definitions relate to this study in particular and may not be universally accepted.

aggregator   Any third party (i.e. not the publisher or client) who distributes a dataset, or arranges for it to be distributed (including bundle deals).

authentication   The means by which a publisher or supplier can discriminate between legitimate users and those not allowed access to the product.

bundle   A deal which includes a 'bundle' of titles. This usually is encountered with electronic journals or electronic books where the complete print run of a publisher might be bundled together under a single deal.

collection developer   The person(s) charged with collection development in an institution. In most cases this would be a librarian.

collection development   The acquisition of titles and products which add to a collection. For the purposes of this book it has been divided into traditional or print collection development, and electronic collection development. However, it is argued that both should be considered together as the two are naturally interlinked.

current awareness system	A system, or combination of systems, set up to automatically keep readers up to date in both their subject interests and in emerging technology.
data	The content of a dataset. Data can be text, numerical, image, audio, video, etc.
dataset	Any electronic product that delivers a collection of data, be it text, numerical, graphical, or time based, as a commercially available title.
delivery	The action by which the content of the dataset is made available to the reader. In the case of remote datasets the delivery will be the responsibility of the publisher or aggregator. In the case of locally held datasets it will be the responsibility of the local institution.
desiderata	A wish-list of products that a collection developer would like to buy or subscribe to.
digital	A generic description of anything held in electronic format. Purists would argue that there is a distinction between 'digital' and 'electronic' but for the purposes of this introductory guide the two are used synonymously. Hence 'digital resources' and 'electronic resources' are interchangeable.
disaggregation	The process by which one can select subsets from a series of titles (usually a bundled deal).
e-book	An electronic representation of a book. In this discussion this refers to a title such as a textbook, but not a reference work.
e-book reader	The electronic device (hardware or software) needed to read an e-book.
e-information	The International Coalition of Library Consortia's term for a dataset.

e-journal   An electronic resource published as a serial, often duplicating a journal that already exists in print form, but also occasionally being born digital.

interface   The front-end screen via which a reader accesses the dataset or collection of datasets.

linkage   In the context of electronic resources, this refers to linking between one dataset and another (i.e. an A&I service linking to full-text versions of the articles, or cross-referencing between products).

local   An indication of the location of a dataset or other function. It is termed 'local' because it is the responsibility of the local institution.

migration   The moving of data from one format to another. For example, a digital image might be migrated from a JPEG image to a TIFF image (as the latter is considered a better archival format).

mirrors   Copies ('reflections') of the original source item that the user wishes to look at. This can be an entire dataset or a piece of software.

print   Any resource that relies on print as the storage mechanism. See also **traditional**.

publication   Any title or collection of titles produced as a single entity. Publications in this book can be both traditional and electronic.

publisher   The body responsible for creating the dataset or publication.

push/pull technology   In push technology the information is sent out to the user with minimal effort on their part. With pull technology the user has to retrieve the information.

reader

Those, also known as users, who will make active use of the datasets bought or subscribed to.

remote

An indication of the location of a dataset or other function. It is termed 'remote' because it is distanced in some way (either physically or by responsibility) from the local institution.

stakeholders

The person(s) or bodies that will be directly affected by any collection-development decisions at the local institution (i.e. not including publishers or suppliers).

standalone

A reference to the fact that the dataset has to be loaded onto an individual machine and can only be accessed by a single user at any one time (i.e. it is not networked).

supplier

The body responsible for selling (and in some cases delivering) the dataset to the collection developer and the readers. Sometimes the supplier is also the publisher, but at other times it is a third-party aggregator.

technical contacts

A term often used for a nominated person at a local institution to receive all information related to a specific dataset.

textbase

A large collection of electronic texts. Because of their long history, and their differences with relation to the new types of e-books, reference works are also included in this definition.

traditional

A term that is used throughout this book to refer to the way things were before the digital revolution. Hence 'traditional collection development' refers to the acquiring and delivering of print-based titles, for example, and 'traditional resources' means anything in non-digital format (printed books and jour-

	nals, paper-based photographs, audio cassettes, and so on).
turn-away	An unsuccessful attempt by a reader to access a dataset because, for example, the number of permitted simultaneous users has been exceeded.
umbrella product	A single-title product which actually includes several titles.
user	See **reader**.

Select bibliography

Journals and e-mail lists

ARL-EJOURNAL Forum
   www.cni.org/Hforums/arl–ejournal

The Charleston Advisor
   www.charlestonco.com/

Computers in Libraries
   www.infotoday.com/cilmag/ciltop.htm

Current Cites
   http://sunsite.berkeley.edu/CurrentCites/

D-Lib Magazine
   www.dlib.org/dlib.html

e-collections@jiscmail.ac.uk

EContent Magazine
   www.ecmag.net/

Information Research
   http://InformationR.net/ir/

Information World Review
   www.iwr.co.uk/iwr/

Internet Library for Librarians
   www.itcompany.com/inforetriever/

Internet Resources Newsletter (Heriot Watt University)
   www.hw.ac.uk/libwww/irn/

Issues in Science and Technology Librarianship
   www.library.ucsb.edu/istl/)

See especially 'Collection development in the internet age', (Spring, 2001)

www.library.ucsb.edu/istl/01-spring/

Journal of Digital Information

http://jodi.ecs.soton.ac.uk/

Journal of Documentation

www.aslib.co.uk/jdoc/

Journal of Electronic Publishing

www.press.umich.edu/jep/

Learned Publishing

www.learned-publishing.org

Liblicense

www.library.yale.edu/~llicense/index.shtml

Lis-e-books@jiscmail.ac.uk

LITA Newsletter (Libraries and Information Technology Association)

www.lita.org/newslett/index.html

Managing Information

www.managinginformation.com/

Online Information Review

www.emerald-library.com/oir.htm

Online Magazine

www.onlineinc.com/onlinemag/index.html

PACSP (Public Access Computer Systems: Publications)

http://info.lib.uh.edu/pacsp.html

RLG DigiNews

www.rlg.org/preserv/diginews/

Searcher

www.infotoday.com/searcher/default.htm

Articles, monographs and reports

AcqWeb, *Collection development sites*

http://acqweb.library.vanderbilt.edu/acqweb/lis_cd.html

AcqWeb, *Online information vendors and electronic publishers*

http://acqweb.library.vanderbilt.edu/acqweb/pubr/online.html

Arizona Public Libraries, *Collection development training*
   www.dlapr.lib.az.us/cdt/
Arms, C. (1999) *Enabling access in digital libraries* (CLIR)
   www.clir.org/pubs/reports/arms-79/contents.html
Armstrong, C. J. *Collection management and scholarly electronic publishing resource: web bibliography*, Information Automation Limited.
   www.i-a-l.co.uk/CM_Bibl.htm
Aslib (2000) *The Aslib directory of information sources in the United Kingdom*, 11th edn, Aslib.
Aslib (The Association for Information Management)
   www.aslib.com/
Association of Research Libraries (USA) (1997) *Principles for licensing electronic resources*
   www.arl.org/scomm/licensing/principles.html
Atherton, N. (2001) Electronic content via the internet: access and exploitation, *Managing Information* (Jan/Feb), 65.
Bailey, C. W. *Scholarly electronic publishing bibliography*
   http://info.lib.uh.edu/sepb/sepb.html
Baldwin, C. M. and Mitchell, S. (1996) Collection issues and overview, *Untangling the Web Conference*
   www.library.ucsb.edu/untangle/baldwin.html
Chapman, L. (2001) *Managing acquisitions*, Library Association Publishing.
Chronicle of Higher Education (2001) *Technology and the future of academic libraries: a live discussion with Nicholson Baker*, Colloquy Live
   http://chronicle.com/colloquylive/2001/05/library/
Clayton, P. and Gorman, G. E. (2001) *Managing information resources in libraries*, Library Association Publishing.
Cornell University Library, *Digital futures plan*
   www.library.cornell.edu/staffweb/
   CULDigitalFuturesPlan.html
Davis, T. L. (1997) The evolution of selection activities for electronic resources, *Library Trends*, **45** (3), 391–404.
Dickinson, G. K. (1994) *Selection and evaluation of electronic resources*, Libraries Unlimited, Inc.
Dworaczek, M. *Electronic sources of information: a bibliography*

http://library.usask.ca/~dworacze/BIBLIO.HTM
[exhaustive list of publishers, acronyms and articles]

Dworaczek, M. *Subject index to literature on electronic sources of information*
http://library.usask.ca/~dworacze/SUB_INT.HTM

Eason, K., Richardson, S. and Yu, L. (2000) Patterns of use of electronic journals, *Journal of Documentation*, **56** (5), 477–504.

Electronic Collections Coordinating Group, National Library of Canada (1998) *Networked electronic publications policy and guidelines*, October
www.nlc-bnc.ca/918/index-e.html

Emory University General Libraries, *Collection development policy: electronic formats*
http://academic.uofs.edu/organization/codes/emory.html

eprints.org
www.eprints.org/
[free archiving of research material; the site also contains very useful links to discussions in this area. See also the *Open Archives Initiative*
www.openarchives.org/]

Evans, G. E. (2000) *Developing library and information center collections*, 4th edn, Libraries Unlimited.

Faulkner, L. A. and Hahn, K. L. (2001) Selecting electronic publications: the development of a genre statement, *Issues in Science and Technology Librarianship*, Spring.
www.library.ucsb.edu/istl/01-spring/article1.html
[the authors also point to several examples of 'genre statements' or collection policy documents, such as the University of Maryland Libraries' *Collection development policy statement: electronic publications*
www.lib.umd.edu/CLMD/COLL.Policies/epubguide.html]

Flaxbart, D. (2001) Collection development in the internet age: an introduction, *Issues in Science and Technology Librarianship*, Spring.
www.library.ucsb.edu/istl/01-spring/intro.html

Gregor, V. L. (2000) *Selecting and managing electronic resources: a how-to-do-it manual for librarians*, Neal-Schuman Publishers.

Haar, J. (1990) Choosing CD-ROM products, *College and Research Libraries News*, **51** (9), 839–41.

Hanka, R. and Fuka, K. (2000) Information overload and 'just-in-time' knowledge, *The Electronic Library*, **18** (4), 279-84.

Harnard, S., *E-Print archive*

www.cogsci.soton.ac.uk/~harnad/

[various publications and initiatives on the site are of interest especially with relation to e-journals, open archives, etc.]

Harvard University Library, DigAcqweb

http://hul.harvard.edu/digacq/

Henty, M. (2000) *A guide to the collection assessment process*, National Library of Australia

www.nla.gov.au/libraries/help/guide.html

Holleman, C. (2000) Electronic resources: are basic criteria for the selection of material changing?, *Library Trends*, **48** (4), 694–710.

Hsieh-Yee, I. (2000) *Organizing audiovisual and electronic resources for access: a cataloging guide*, Libraries Unlimited.

Humanities and Social Sciences Federation of Canada (2001) *The credibility of electronic publishing*

http://web.mala.bc.ca/hssfc/Final/Credibility.htm

InformationR.net, Digital information in the Information Research field

http://InformationR.net/fr/freejnls.html

[includes an extensive bibliography of online journals]

International Coalition of Library Consortia (1998a) *Guidelines for statistical measures of usage of web-based indexes, abstracted, and full text resources*

www.library.yale.edu/consortia/webstats.html

International Coalition of Library Consortia (1998b) *Statement of current perspective and preferred practices for the selection and purchase of electronic information*

www.library.yale.edu/consortia/statement.html

ISBD(ER): International Standard Bibliographic Description for Electronic Resources

http://ifla.inist.fr/VII/s13/pubs/isbd.htm

Jenkins, C. and Morley, M. (1999) *Collection management in academic libraries,* Gower.

JISC (Joint Information Systems Committee), *Resource guides*

www.jisc.ac.uk/subject/

[lists various collections of interest to specific subject areas].

Johnson, P. (1996) Selecting electronic resources: developing a local decision-making matrix, *Cataloging and Classification Quarterly*, **22** (3–4), 9–24.

Johnson P. (1997) Collection development policies and electronic information resources. In Gorman, G. E. and Miller, R. H. (eds), *Collection management for the 21st century*, Greenwood Press, 83–104.

Joint Steering Committee for Revision of Anglo-American Cataloguing Rules
www.nlc-bnc.ca/jsc/

JUSTEIS: JISC Usage Surveys: Trends in Electronic Information Services
www.dil.aber.ac.uk/dils/Research/JUSTEIS/JISCTop. htm

Kidd, T. and Prior, A. (2000) The acquisition of serials. In Kidd, T. and Rees-Jones, L. (eds) (2000) *The serials management handbook: a practical guide to print and electronic serials management*, Library Association Publishing [in association with the United Kingdom Serials Group], 79–103.

Kidd, T. and Rees-Jones, L. (eds) (2000) *The serials management handbook: a practical guide to print and electronic serials management*, Library Association Publishing [in association with the United Kingdom Serials Group].

Kovacs, D. (2000) *Building electronic library collections: the essential guide to selection criteria and core subject collections*, Neal-Schuman Publishers.

Lancaster, F. W. (1995) The evolution of electronic publishing, *Library Trends*, **43** (4), 518–27.

Laurence, H. and Miller, W. (2000) *Academic research on the internet: options for scholars and librarians*, Haworth Information Press.

Lee, S. D. (2000) *Digital imaging: a practical handbook*, Library Association Publishing.

Lee, S. H. (ed.) (1999) *Collection development in the electronic environment: shifting priorities*, Haworth Information Press.

LAMIT: The Multimedia Information and Technology Group of The Library Association
www.la-hq.org.uk/groups/lamit/

Library of Congress, *Announcement of draft interim guidelines for cataloguing electronic resources*

http://lcweb.loc.gov/catdir/cpso/elec_res.html

Liew, C. L., Foo, S. and Chennupati, K. R. (2000) A study of graduate end-users' use and perception of e-journals, *Online Information Review*, **24** (4), 302–15.

Luther, J. (2000) *White paper on electronic journal usage statistics*, Council on Library and Information Resources
www.clir.org/pubs/abstract/pub94abst.html

McKnight, C. and Price, S. (1999) A survey of author attitudes and skills in relation to article publishing in paper and electronic journals, *Journal of Documentation*, **55** (5), 556–76.

Meadows, J. (2000) Why do we need serials? In Kidd, T. and Rees-Jones, L. (eds) *The serials management handbook: a practical guide to print and electronic serials management*, Library Association Publishing [in association with the United Kingdom Serials Group], 1–15.

Metz, P. (2000) Principles of selection for electronic resources, *Library Trends*, **48** (4), 711–29.

Meyers, B. (1996) Electronic publishing: a brief history and some current activities, *IP News*, Fall.
www.knotworks.com/IPNews/pub/1996.4.
EpubHistAndCurrent.html

MIMAS: Manchester Information and Associated Services
www.superjournal.ac.uk

Morris, S. (2000) How and why serials are produced. In Kidd, T. and Rees-Jones, L. (eds) (2000) *The serials management handbook: a practical guide to print and electronic serials management*, Library Association Publishing [in association with the United Kingdom Serials Group], 16–41.

Moskowitz, R. (2001) What is a virtual private network?, *Network Computing*
www.networkcomputing.com/905/905colmoskowitz. html

National Electronic Site Licence Initiative (NESLI)
www.nesli.ac.uk/
[contains the NESLI model licence
www.nesli.ac.uk/ModelLicence8a.html
based on the draft document formulated by the UK's Publishers Association and JISC; in the US there is the CLIR/DLF equivalent

www.library.yale.edu/~llicense/modlic.shtml]

Nature, Future e-access to the primary literature

www.nature.com/nature/debates/e-access/index.html

[See also *Science*

www.sciencemag.org/cgi/eletters/291/5512/2318a

and *American Scientist's* September 1998 archive

http://amsci-forum.amsci.org/archives/september98-forum.html]

Okerson, A. *Electronic collections development*

www.library.yale.edu/~okerson/ecd.html

[list of links to various collection-development statements by many of the major research and public libraries]

Okerson, A. (1996) Buy or lease? Two models for scholarly information at the end (or the beginning) of an era, *Daedalus: Journal of the American Academy of Arts and Sciences*, **125** (4), 55–76; see also

www.library.yale.edu/~okerson/daedalus.html

Olson, N. B. (ed.) *Cataloging internet resources*, OCLC

www.oclc.org/oclc/man/9256cat/toc.htm

On-Line Information Annual Conference; see 2001 Conference site at

www.online-information.co.uk/online/

Ormes, S. (ed.) (2000) *An e-book primer: an issue paper from the Networked Services Policy Taskgroup*, UKOLN (on behalf of EARL, The Library Association and UKOLN.

www.ukoln.ac.uk/public/earl/issuepapers/ebook.htm

Oxford University, *Cataloguing electronic resources*

www.bodley.ox.ac.uk/dept/techserv/ulstst/catsig/docs/eresources/cataloguing.pdf

Pedley, P. (2001) Electronic journals, *Managing Information*, (Jan/Feb), 61.

PURCEL (2000) *Purchasing decisions of electronic resources in higher education instititions*

www.library.sunderland.ac.uk/jisc/Final%20report.pdf

Rowland, F., McKnight, C. and Meadows, J. (eds) (1995) *Project ELVYN: an experiment in electronic journal delivery*, Bowker-Saur.

Rowley, J. (2000) *JISC user behaviour monitoring and evaluation framework . . . August 2000*

www.jisc.ac.uk/pub00/m&e_rep1.html

Royal Society of Chemistry, *RSC Electronic information licence agreement*
www.rsc.org/is/journals/current/ej_use.htm

Scholarly Publishing and Academic Resources Coalition (SPARC)
www.arl.org/sparc/
[a major e-journal initiative launched by the research community]

Slagell, J. (2001) The good, the bad, and the ugly: evaluating electronic journals, *Computers in Libraries*, **21** (5) (May), 34–8.

Stephens, A. (1998) *Public library collection development in the information age*, Haworth Press.

Stewart, L. A. (2000) Choosing between print and electronic resources: the selection dilemma, *The Reference Librarian*, **71**, 79–97.

Thomas Parry Library, University of Wales, Aberystwyth, *Electronic journals in librarianship and information science*
www.info.aber.ac.uk/tpl/ejlib/

Tilburg University (1997) *Licensing principles: guidelines and checklist for libraries*
http://cwis.kub.nl/~dbi/english/license/licprinc.htm

UK Mirror Service
www.mirror.ac.uk/
[see also the Service's newsletter, *The Looking Glass*
www.mirror.ac.uk/help/news/index.html

University of California Libraries (1996) *Principles for acquiring and licensing information in digital formats*
http://sunsite.berkeley.edu/Info/principles.html

Virtual Private Network Consortium
www.vpnc.org/

Watkinson, A. (2001) *Electronic solutions to the problems of monograph publishing*, PA
www.publishers.org.uk/

Weihs, J. R. (1991) *The integrated library: encouraging access to multimedia materials*, 2nd edn, Oryx Press.

Weintraub, J. (1998) The development and use of a genre statement for electronic journals in the sciences, *Issues in Science and Technology Librarianship*, Winter
www.library.ucsb.edu/istl/98-winter/article5.html

Weitz, J. (2000) *Cataloging electronic resources: OCLC-MARC coding guidelines*
www.oclc.org/oclc/cataloging/type.htm

Woodward, H., Rowland, J. F., McKnight, C., Pritchett, C. and Meadows, A. J. (1998) Cafe Jus: an electronic journals user study, *Journal of Digital Information*, **1** (3)
http://jodi.ecs.soton.ac.uk/Articles/v01/i03/Woodward/

Working Group of the Conference of Directors of National Libraries (1996) *The legal deposit of electronic publications*, Unesco
www.unesco.org/webworld/memory/legaldep.htm

Xie, H. and Cool, C. (2000) Ease of use versus user control: an evaluation of web and non-web interfaces on online databases, *Online Information Review*, **24** (2), 102–15.

Yin Zhang (2001) Scholarly use of internet-based electronic resources, *Journal of the American Society for Information Science and Technology*, **52** (8).

Index